A
UNITED
IRELAND

A

UNITED
IRELAND

KEVIN MEAGHER

/BP/

A UNITED IRELAND

WHY UNIFICATION IS INEVITABLE AND HOW IT WILL COME ABOUT

KEVIN MEAGHER

Biteback Publishing

First published in Great Britain in 2016 by
Biteback Publishing Ltd
Westminster Tower
3 Albert Embankment
London SE1 7SP
Copyright © Kevin Meagher 2016

ISBN 978-1-78590-172-0

10 9 8 7 6 5 4 3 2 1

A CIP catalogue record for this book is available from the British Library.

Set in Kepler by Adrian McLaughlin

Printed and bound in Great Britain by
CPI Group (UK) Ltd, Croydon CR0 4YY

Undoubtedly, this book will divide opinion. For each person who finds themselves in agreement with the arguments I set out, there will be another who strongly disagrees.

The point, however, is to generate debate. To open up a discussion that has lain dormant for too long. To set out the truth as I see it. Others may have theirs.

But what is surely beyond contention is that Brexit, the ongoing threat of a Scottish breakaway and the growth of provincial English centres of power present very real challenges to Northern Ireland's place in the United Kingdom. Quite apart from the compelling empirical evidence that Irish unity now makes overwhelming economic sense.

In the time-honoured tradition, any omissions or inaccuracies over subsequent pages remain entirely my own.

For Lucy, Elizabeth and James. And my mum and dad.

CONTENTS

INTRODUCTION

I n writing this book, let me begin by explaining what it is not. It is not a history book. Clearly, when delving into the political affairs of Ireland, it is impossible for historical events not to play a significant part. Quite unavoidably, they soak into every page, serving as context for the present. It is not my intention, however, to provide the reader with a comprehensive history either of Ireland or of the Troubles. Where I have employed historical facts I have done so to illuminate and set in context my specific argument about the inevitability of Irish reunification.

Neither have I embarked on a work of political science. Northern Ireland has a burgeoning and erudite community of academics who pore over every event and nuance there in impeccably recorded detail. My intention is not to look at Northern Ireland through a telescope but, rather, to take a step back and gaze at the panorama.

This book is intended to be an extended political argument. The aim is to raise questions that have remained unasked and unheard (and perhaps, even, unthought) in British politics for too long. I am trying to encourage a discussion about the most basic issues in relation to Northern Ireland. Why are we still there? Will we ever leave? What are the circumstances that could propel us to do so? And what arrangements would we put in place instead?

And when I use the royal 'we' I mean Britain, or, more precisely, the British political class. This is a book about British politics. I am trying to assess the issues involved in terms of what they mean for the British public and British public debate. This is something of a rarity. Northern Ireland seldom comes up. We are not much interested in what goes on there and don't really think about the place – a somewhat anomalous situation given the governance of Ireland and latterly Northern Ireland is probably the longest-running fault line in British politics.

Indeed, the 'Irish Question' (or, more often, the Irish 'problem') has dogged British politics, in one form or another, since at least the time of the 1800 Act of Union and the abolition of the Irish Parliament (if not for centuries before that), as the British state struggled (and, more often than not, failed) to establish a popular mandate to govern the Irish. It is a question/problem that has rolled on into the modern age. During the last three decades of the twentieth century, it took the form of the Northern Ireland 'Troubles' (an epic piece of understatement for what amounted to a major secessionist uprising that cost the lives of 3,600 people) and although the past twenty years have seen intensive efforts to secure a devolved local settlement via the Good Friday Agreement, the constitutional status of Northern Ireland remains moot.

How could it not? A canter through British–Irish relations over much of the last millennium tells a grisly tale of invasion, subjugation, ethnic cleansing, famine, disease, insurrection, counter-insurrection, retreats, partial victories and brooding stalemates. The province of Northern Ireland was created as a back-foot political compromise in order to split the difference between Republicans vying for national self-determination and Loyalists set on having their identity and local hegemony rewarded.

Yet, here we are, nine decades on, still in possession of the north-east corner of the island of Ireland – six counties of the historic province of Ulster – long past the point when there is any rational reason to remain. Rational, certainly, from the perspective of the people of Great Britain. We have paid a heavy price in both blood and treasure for the failures of successive governments to oversee the British state's orderly retreat from its oldest colony, a faraway land of which we know and seemingly care little about.

Now, two decades' worth of incremental political progress is creating space in which the long-term future of Northern Ireland can and should be openly discussed. Part of this involves rehabilitating the concept of Irish unity as the most logical endpoint. This is not, *per se*, to echo Irish Republican arguments, merely to articulate the most obvious destination of the current direction of travel.

Physically, socially and politically remote from the rest of the UK and unviable as an economic entity in its own right, Northern Ireland's endurance for nearly 100 years is merely testament to the indolence of a British political class that has been content to keep the place at arm's length.

While the principle of consent – that there should be no change in Northern Ireland's constitutional status without the consent of the majority who live there – was hardwired into the Good Friday Agreement settlement in 1998, it also effectively placed Northern Ireland in an antechamber. If there is, eventually, a majority of people living there who consent to change its constitutional status, the British and Irish governments will facilitate that desire. Nowhere else is Britain so sanguine about sovereignty and it is impossible to imagine in this scenario that, a few ultras apart, the British political class would lift a finger to persuade Northern Ireland to stay in any future referendum campaign on its constitutional status.

Nevertheless, there is a responsibility to be honest about where things may end up. Although political developments in relation to Northern Ireland are usually glacial, the potential value from closer economic integration between the northern and southern parts of the island of Ireland means that the politics will have to catch up sooner rather than later. Equally, demographic and cultural changes in Northern Ireland mean traditionally Nationalist Catholics will probably outnumber traditionally Protestant Unionists within a decade at the most (while the spectre of 'Catholic Ireland' is hardly a potent bogeyman in a country that became the first in the world to legalise gay marriage in a referendum in May 2015). This is quite apart from broader issues that may force a reshaping of the United Kingdom from first principles – specifically, the impacts of Brexit, devolution to conurbations within England and the prospect of a second referendum on Scottish independence within the next decade. To put it bluntly, there may not be a United Kingdom for Unionists to be loyal to.

None of the arguments or analyses put forward is intended to disregard the moral and historical legitimacy of advocating the reunification of

Ireland. This book is, though, advancing the proposition that history is propelled along by lots of small strokes of the oar. It is not by grand gestures or dramatic events that a united Ireland will come about, but by the kinds of piecemeal, utilitarian developments that I try to chronicle in subsequent pages.

The arguments I set out to propound in this book are, I think, timely given Northern Ireland is rarely written about or discussed from the British perspective. It is surely right that we ceased to be inhibited from debating what kind of relationship we want to see with our nearest neighbour and trading partner and openly explored the alternatives that best suit the British people, especially when taxpayers pick up a £9 billion annual bill for maintaining Northern Ireland and face lingering security risks associated with the current, faltering, status quo.

Clearly, at the moment, a majority of Northern Ireland's inhabitants currently wish to remain part of Britain. They are entitled to that view: after all, they live there. But that percentage is shrinking and the days when Unionists could exert a veto on political developments they do not like are surely over. It is entirely legitimate for other voices and different perspectives to now come to the fore, articulating new visions for the future and new models of governing the island of Ireland. Respecting the consent principle is not and should not be a conversation-stopper.

Yet, for too long, British politics has observed a self-denying ordinance from openly discussing what future constitutional arrangements best suit the British people. The relief that the Troubles are over is palpable and there is little interest in doing or saying anything that disturbs this fragile settlement, hence the lack of honest discussion.

This book is a modest attempt to stimulate that debate. It will explore the historical context – how we have ended up where we are and why – before moving on to discuss how different Northern Ireland is to the rest of the UK; the role of economics in driving an all-Ireland dimension; the mood of the Irish Republic towards the question of unity; how the once-difficult relationship between Britain and Ireland has been transformed in recent years, providing a stable context for any change of sovereignty over the north; and offer an examination of the scenarios in which British political elites will be presented with a compelling case for Irish unity in the years to come, whether or not they choose to drive the agenda.

KEVIN MEAGHER

Summer 2016

CHAPTER ONE

WHY WE ARE
WHERE WE ARE

I t is quite impossible to write anything about Ireland without providing the reader with an historical *precis*. The trouble comes in deciding where to begin. There is so much history, so much context, so much political strife, that it's comparable to explaining *Coronation Street* from the very beginning to a visiting Martian. Do we start with Strongbow? The Flight of the Earls? The Ulster plantation? Cromwell? The suspension of the Irish Parliament? Wolfe Tone? The Fenians? Easter 1916? The War of Independence? Partition? The Irish Civil War? The sheer scale of it, to the uninitiated, which, in this case, is pretty much everyone in Britain, is bamboozling.

But it all matters. Each tumultuous event in Irish history, those mentioned above and dozens more besides, feed into one another, becoming symbiotic as one failed uprising against British rule simply inspires a repeat event. Each atrocity committed by the British state resulting in a backlash. Each rising being put down. Historical grievances echo down the generations. But what remains, the cause of so much history and angst, is, at the root of it, an incredibly simple issue: should Britain rule Ireland or not?

The fraught relationship between Britain and Ireland dates from the twelfth-century Norman invasion, beginning a sequence of rebellions, truces, stalemates, further rebellions, repressions and yet more rebellions that stretches into the modern era. The ambitious English King, Henry II, set foot in Ireland in 1171 and, although he secured bases in the east of Ireland, he did not manage to dominate the country. A century later, a Gaelic revival undermined the Norman conquest, aided by military victories for the native Gaels and the impact of the Black Death (which hit the Normans harder as they lived in towns while the rural Irish were more sparsely populated). England's grip on Ireland weakened and was reduced to the fortified parts of Dublin on the east coast known as the Pale, with its writ not running in the rest of the country ('beyond the Pale').

Under Henry VIII, there was a more concerted attempt to force Ireland's submission. Wary of Ireland being used as a backdoor to strike against England, Henry prosecuted a typically bloody campaign to centralise control under the Crown, but was less successful in converting the native Irish to Protestantism. So, in order to consolidate their advances (and to avoid a similar fate to the Normans), lands were confiscated and a loyal garrison from England and Scotland would be brought to Ireland as part of the policy of 'plantation'. Sectarianism had arrived. In order to bolster this new Protestant ascendancy in Ireland, a series of Penal Laws were introduced with the intention of killing off Catholicism altogether. They included a ban on Catholics sitting in the Irish Parliament, voting,

3

practising law or serving as officers in the army or navy. Catholics were not allowed their own schools, or to send their children abroad for their education. They could not marry Protestants and any priest who did so faced death for his trouble. Catholic bishops were banned from the country (on pain of death) and priests needed to be registered (failure to do so saw them branded on the cheek). No Catholic could own a horse with a value of more than five pounds. (Ingeniously, this law allowed a Protestant the right to buy any horse from any Catholic for that amount.) The philosopher Edmund Burke described the system of Penal Laws as 'a machine of wise and elaborate contrivance, as well fitted for the oppression, impoverishment and degradation of a people, and the debasement in them of human nature itself, as ever proceeded from the perverted ingenuity of man'.

It's fair to say the Tudors left their mark on Ireland. In English folklore, Sir Walter Raleigh is famed for the apocryphal and entirely benign tale that he laid his cloak over a puddle for Elizabeth I to walk across. In Irish history, he is remembered as an English officer responsible for the massacre of 700 Spanish and Italian troops at the Siege of Smerwick in County Kerry in 1580. The soldiers, part of a Papal force sent to assist the Irish nobles resisting English rule, found themselves cut off and surrendered. Despite assurances to the contrary, every last man (with the exception of a few officers) was killed. Raleigh's reward was 4,000 acres of Irish land.

Throughout the sixteenth and seventeenth centuries, English control of Ireland waxed and waned. Periodic bouts of rebellion actually led to the creation of the Irish Catholic Confederation, a seven-year period between 1642 and 1649 during which the Irish Catholic nobles and clergy governed their own affairs through an assembly in Kilkenny. This flame of freedom was snuffed out when Oliver Cromwell began his conquest of Ireland in 1649. There is surely no figure in British and Irish history that so divides opinion in these isles. Parliament saw fit to erect a statue of Cromwell outside the House of Commons, a hero of parliamentary democracy against the rule of kings. For the Irish, Cromwell is a butcher. An ethnic cleanser. A tyrant.

His notoriety was well-earned. Landing in Ireland in 1649 with a force of 20,000 troops, Cromwell crushed all opposition before him, ordering the execution of more than 3,500 men, women and children loyal to King Charles I in Drogheda. The bloodlust continued in Wexford and a similar massacre ensued. After that, word of his atrocities spread and opposition crumbled. It allowed Cromwell to seize the assets of the Catholic Church and sack its churches and monasteries. Catholic landowners were dispossessed and forcibly relocated to Connaught, Ireland's westernmost province (and, in agricultural terms, its least propitious). 'To Hell or to Connaught' was the choice. Cromwell's officers were paid in confiscated land, which many sold to the English and Scottish gentry, creating a class of absentee landlords. To top it off, Cromwell sold off defeated soldiers, women and children, exiling them to the West Indies.

The restoration of the monarchy in 1660 under Charles II brought little relief for the Irish. The one thing uniting roundhead and cavalier, parliamentarian and monarchist, was utter contempt for them. In 1685, James II came to the throne. As a convert to Catholicism, Protestants feared the beginning of a Catholic restoration. Lord Danby, leader of the Whigs, encouraged James's son-in-law, the Dutch prince William of Orange, to rise up against him. James was forced to flee to France before heading for Ireland in the hope of rallying support there to regain the throne. In 1690, his Jacobite army faced William's at the River Boyne in County Meath in southern Ireland. Outnumbered and outclassed by William's professional soldiers, James was defeated, again taking refuge in France from his seriously estranged son-in-law. (Reliving William's success at the Battle of the Boyne remains the high point of the Orange Order's annual calendar.) William was eventually halted at Limerick by the well-organised Irish general, Patrick Sarsfield, who forced him to agree to terms in exchange for disbanding his army. The Treaty of Limerick of 1691 was to see religious freedom and the rights of the native Irish restored, while Sarsfield's army went into exile, forming Irish brigades in many Continental armies (somewhere in the region of half a million Irishmen – so-called 'wild geese' – would do the same over the next century, denied, by the Penal Laws, the right to serve in the British Army). Sarsfield kept his part of the bargain. The English Parliament, however, did not.

By the late eighteenth century, only 5 per cent of Irish land was owned by Catholics, even though they made up three-quarters of the population. The ongoing and unjust effects of the Penal Laws led to a further rebellion. The Society of United Irishmen, led by Theobald Wolfe Tone, a Kildare lawyer, took inspiration from the American War of Independence and the French Revolution to champion a non-sectarian, independent Irish Republic, uniting 'Catholic, Protestant and Dissenter'. His call found a ready audience among Catholics, but also Presbyterians (who were also subject to the Penal Laws, although not as harshly dealt with as Catholics). A rising in 1798 led by Tone was eventually put down and Prime Minister William Pitt moved to abolish the Irish Parliament and make Ireland part of the United Kingdom. The Act of Union became law in 1801. For his part, Tone is still revered as a theorist-martyr, providing an intellectual lodestar for contemporary Irish Republicans who seek to emulate his call for national self-determination on the basis of equality and liberty for all.

In 1823, another young lawyer tried different tactics. Daniel O'Connell formed the Catholic Association to campaign for an end to the Penal Laws and to improve the lot of impoverished tenant farmers. It soon became a mass movement, advocating non-violence, and successfully fused together the peasant Irish and the Catholic Church. The Association began to win a series of parliamentary by-elections and, sensing the increasing political danger, Prime Minister Arthur Wellesley, the Duke of Wellington, introduced a Catholic Relief Bill in 1829, removing most of the institutionalised discrimination facing Catholics in both Ireland and Britain. At the same time, however, he introduced legislation to remove the franchise from many small farmers, the bedrock of the Association's support.

As a pioneer of non-violent, mass mobilisation in order to secure political change, O'Connell – 'the Liberator' – next turned his efforts to repealing the Act of Union itself, with a series of 'monster meetings' at historical sites across the country. These were gatherings in the hundreds of thousands, culminating in a meeting in Cashel where up to a million people were said to have attended. A larger gathering still planned for Tara was banned by the authorities. Given O'Connell had been careful to keep his activities within the law, he cancelled the meeting, and, now aged seventy, political power drained away from him and toward more militant efforts for national self-determination.

Throughout the nineteenth century, efforts to obtain Irish freedom oscillated between constitutional agitation and attempts to remove Britain by force. From the mid-nineteenth century onwards, Irish affairs began to feature heavily in British politics (owing to the scrapping of the Irish Parliament and the presence of Irish MPs in the House of Commons). In 1844, there was a nine-day 'great debate' in the House of Commons on a motion put forward by Lord John Russell on the proposition that 'Ireland is occupied not governed'. The motion was defeated but the symbolism that Ireland was a place apart, a perennial problem that needed resolving, was founded in British politics. The 'Irish Question' was born. British politics was going through a relatively progressive phase at the time, but as the historian D. G. Boyce puts it: '...the British belief in reasonable government, consensus and fair play, even if dismissed as typical of hypocritical Albion, could and did prove embarrassing to a British government bent on enforcing "firmness" in Ireland'.

If parliamentarians thought Ireland was a problem in 1844, the following year would reveal just how big the scale of that problem was. So began *An Gorta Mor* – 'the Great Hunger', a famine that would, over coming years, ravage Ireland, cutting its population in half, leaving a million souls to die terrible deaths from starvation and typhoid, while a million more were forced to emigrate. Many say the numbers in both instances are higher. The virulent potato blight, *Phytophthora infestans*, carried on the wind and washed down into the soil, turned the potato crop, the staple diet of the peasant Irish, into putrid mush. Given the particular model of agrarian capitalism in Ireland, with its absentee English landlords and compartmentalised plots of land, the hardy potato was the only realistic crop that could be grown by subsistence farmers.

The effects of the blight were immediate and severe. Relief, when it came, was partial and inadequate. The civil servant in charge of the relief effort, Sir Charles Trevelyan, an evangelical Christian and ardent disciple of *laissez faire*, believed that 'the judgement of God sent the calamity to teach the Irish a lesson'. Such was the famine's scale that the *Times* newspaper remarked that 'a Celtic Irishman' would become 'as rare in Connemara as is the Red Indian on the shores of Manhattan'. The Lord Lieutenant of Ireland, George Villiers, the Earl of Clarendon (whose descendant, Theresa Villiers, served as David Cameron's Northern Ireland Secretary), wrote to Prime Minister Lord John Russell beseeching him to intervene and avert this 'policy of extermination'.

This was British 'firmness' in action. The Irish had brought this on themselves and could not expect Britain to bail them out. Help, when it came, had strings. The Church of Ireland offered food aid to those who would renounce their Catholicism.

'Taking the soup' became the insult aimed at those who did. Queen Victoria was so 'moved' she offered the trifling amount of £1,000 worth of relief. Hearing about the plight of the Irish, the Sultan of the Ottoman Empire offered £10,000, only to have the British government ask him to reduce it so it didn't embarrass the Queen. (The story goes that he still sent three ships laden with food aid surreptitiously.) In an equally remarkable gesture, the Native American Choctaw tribe raised money for the starving Irish. As displaced people themselves, they empathised with the 'Trail of Tears' the Irish now found themselves on.

The memory of those years, the sheer scale of death and suffering, as well as the dislocation inflicted on that generation of the Irish people, is seared into the collective memory of all subsequent generations. Of course, this being Ireland, it was not the first time the people had been left to starve by their English masters. The same thing had happened a century earlier. In 1740–41, famine was responsible for killing nearly four in ten of the population of the island (proportionately more severe than the famine of the 1840s). Extreme cold and wet weather destroyed the grain harvests as well as the potato crop. In Ireland, history repeats itself. The first time as tragedy and the second time as tragedy.

The rest of the nineteenth century is zipped between political attempts and militaristic forays to achieve independence via the ballot box or by the musket. The Irish Parliamentary Party of Charles Stewart Parnell and the Land League agitations of Michael Davitt tried the former while the Young Irelanders in the 1840s and the Fenians in the 1860s tried the latter. Despite their different tactics, each served to make Britain's presence in Ireland more alien and the Irish more ungovernable. The one British political figure who stands out during this period was the Grand Old Man himself, William Ewart Gladstone. As the historian D. G. Boyce put it: 'Gladstone believed that, in the case of Ireland at least, politics had a destination, and the Irish Question a solution.'

His efforts at delivering Home Rule for Ireland dominated late Victorian and Edwardian British politics. 'My mission is to pacify Ireland,' he proclaimed at the 1868 general election. Gladstone began by disestablishing the Church of Ireland, serving to underscore the decline of the old Protestant ascendancy. In 1874, the Home Rule League was formed to campaign for a restoration of the Irish Parliament, managing to win half the seats in Ireland (aided, no doubt, by this being the first general election to employ the secret ballot). The next few years were dominated by the question of land reform with poor tenant farmers mobilised under the National Land League, founded by Michael Davitt and headed by MP, Charles Stewart Parnell. The Land League demanded reform of the rotten system whereby absentee landlords could charge extortionate rents and evict tenants on a whim. In one memorable incident, the League's direct action included refusing to harvest the crop of Lord Erne, an absentee landlord, whose agent, a Captain Charles Boycott, subsequently entered the lexicon as a verb.

In 1885, Parnell's Irish Parliamentary Party found itself holding the balance of power in Westminster. The following year, Gladstone brought forward the

first of three Home Rule Bills which was nevertheless defeated at its Second Reading. 'Home Rule
Means Rome Rule' was the cry of opponents; ironic,
given Parnell, like so many Irish Nationalists before
him, was Protestant. Following his death in 1891,
the octogenarian Gladstone brought forward a second Home Rule Bill in 1893. This time it passed its
Commons stages but foundered in the Conservative-
dominated House of Lords.

The first two decades of the twentieth century
brought further tumult. In 1905, Sinn Féin was
formed to campaign more vigorously for Irish sep-
aratism, while at Westminster, Parnell's Irish
Parliamentary Party, now under the leadership of
John Redmond, pursued the constitutional route.
Following the two general elections in 1910, the
Irish once again held the balance of power and used
the advantage to press Asquith's Liberals to bring
forth a third Home Rule Bill. With the Parliament
Act in place, establishing the primacy of the House
of Commons over the House of Lords, the prospect of achieving Home Rule was at last in sight.
In the north, Edward Carson, a Dublin Protestant,

led opposition to it. At this stage, there was no desire to divide the 'Protestant north' from the 'Catholic south'. However, Unionist opposition became increasingly militant, with the formation of the Ulster Volunteer Force (UVF) to forcibly resist Home Rule, if necessary. Conservative opposition leader Andrew Bonar Law told a rally in Belfast: 'I can imagine no length of resistance to which Ulster can go in which I should not be prepared to support it.' To underline their opposition, Unionists established a petition, 'Ulster's Solemn League and Covenant'. So intense was the feeling that some were said to have signed in their own blood.

Nevertheless, the third Home Rule Bill passed its parliamentary stages in September 1914, but was suspended by the outbreak of the First World War. Carson urged the UVF to enlist and they formed the 36th Ulster Division, going on to take heavy casualties at the Battle of the Somme. Redmond similarly urged the Irish to join up to fight for 'the rights of small nations'. Sensing the British had yet again welched on a deal, Irish Republicans saw a chance to drive a preoccupied Britain out of Ireland for good. The Easter Rising of 1916 is, more than any other, the seminal moment in twentieth-century Irish history. An armed insurrection, centred on Dublin, saw rebels take control of strategic buildings and sites across the capital and battle British forces for a week until being forced to surrender. The subsequent treatment of the leaders – courts martial and firing squads for the sixteen leaders – outraged Irish opinion. The days of British rule in Ireland were numbered.

From then on, events became, if anything, more fraught. In 1919, those Irish MPs who had been elected in the previous year's general election refused to sit in Westminster and formed a break-away parliament, Dáil Éireann, to act as a rallying point for the country. A guerrilla war against British rule in Ireland began, with the government dispatching mercenaries to supplement the police and army. Their mismatched uniforms earned them the sobriquet 'Black and Tans' and their notorious barbarity against the civilian population simply hardened the resolve of the Irish against British rule. In Dublin, the IRA's director of intelligence, Michael Collins,

wiped out a network of intelligence agents, assassi-
nating them simultaneously one Sunday morning.
The same day, at a Gaelic football match in Dublin's
Croke Park, British soldiers, ostensibly preparing to
search men leaving the ground, opened fire on the
crowd, killing fourteen people including two boys
aged ten and eleven. The events of 21 November 1920
became known as 'Bloody Sunday'. (Again, Irish history repeats itself and there would be another, even
more infamous, Bloody Sunday to come.) In 1922, a
treaty was negotiated that would see an Irish Free
State established, under the British Empire, while
six counties of the historic province of Ulster would
split off to form Northern Ireland. The treaty was
narrowly supported in the Dáil, although it couldn't
stop civil war breaking out in Ireland between those
for and against it. Eventually Irish Free State forces
prevailed. The treaty was implemented and Northern Ireland went its own way.

The years between partition in 1922 and the suspension of Stormont in 1972 were characterised
by the growth of deep inequalities between Catholics and the numerically superior Protestants of

Northern Ireland. The province's first Prime Minister, James Craig, infamously described Northern Ireland as 'a Protestant Parliament and Protestant State'. The basic premise was that if Catholics didn't like how things were run, they could go and live in the south. The sectarianism was palpable. In 1934, the Unionist Minister of Agriculture (and subsequent Prime Minister), Sir Basil Brooke, was explicit in urging employers 'not to employ Roman Catholics, who were 99 per cent disloyal'. His colleague, Minister of Labour J. M. Andrews, was pleased to respond to a rumour that twenty-eight of the thirty-one porters at Stormont were Roman Catholics. 'I have investigated the matter, and I find that there are thirty Protestants, and only one Roman Catholic, there temporarily.'

These attitudes permeated every corner of the state. Electoral boundaries were gerrymandered to ensure Unionist hegemony wherever possible. This was significant because Northern Ireland was a patchwork of small local authorities. By the late 1960s, there were some seventy-three local authorities for a population of 1.5 million. Crucially, the franchise for local elections was on the basis of property ownership, not universal suffrage. It was estimated that in 1961 over a quarter of the parliamentary electorate were disfranchised at local elections. Moreover, the retention of a company vote entitled business directors to more than one ballot paper. This then allowed housing allocations to be rigged and municipal jobs to go to the 'right' people. Discrimination was built into the fabric of Northern Ireland. It was state-sponsored, all-pervasive and seen to be a reasonable course, channelling generations of ingrained hostility towards Catholics from the Reformation onwards. Meanwhile, the Ulster Special Constabulary, the so-called 'B-Specials', were on hand as a quasi-militaristic, sectarian police force that would achieve notoriety for their brutal baton-wielding at civil rights demonstrations.

The former IRA hunger striker turned playwright Laurence McKeown described his first experience of discrimination when, as a young boy in the 1960s, his father applied to the local council for planning permission to build a bungalow. He was sure the application would be approved because he borrowed a plan that a Protestant colleague of his had previously used successfully. Yet McKeown's father's application was rejected by his local council on no less than thirty-nine grounds. 'It was the first time I saw my father take a stand,' McKeown recounted in an interview with the *Irish Times*. 'He got a lawyer and appealed. The lawyer pointed out the council had passed the exact same plans a couple of years previously. Suddenly all the objections disappeared apart from three face-saving ones. It was only in later years that I realised it was to do with civil rights.'

But even buttoned-up Northern Ireland was not immune from the swinging '60s and found itself pulsating to a modernising beat. A Unionist moderate, Terence O'Neill, became Prime Minister of Northern Ireland in 1963. Captain O'Neill was a moderniser, keen to transcend Unionist and Nationalist identities which had become 'a ludicrous anachronism' that he wanted to replace with 'normal twentieth-century politics based on a division between left and right'. Alas, his good intentions did not inoculate him from the occasional bout of foot-in-mouth disease. Despite believing it made sense to treat the Catholic minority decently, his explanation for doing so was not particularly elegant:

> It is frightfully hard to explain to Protestants that if you give Roman Catholics a good job and a good house they will live like Protestants because they will see neighbours with cars and television sets; they will refuse to have eighteen children. But if a Roman Catholic is jobless, and lives in the most ghastly hovel, he will rear eighteen children on National Assistance. If you treat Roman Catholics with due consideration and kindness, they will live like Protestants in spite of the authoritative nature of their Church...[1]

However, change was in the air. President Kennedy paid a state visit to Ireland in 1963 and the IRA's border campaign (which mainly consisted

---

1 Quoted in the *Belfast Telegraph*, 10 May 1969 (courtesy of the University of Ulster's Conflict Archive on the Internet http://cain.ulst.ac.uk/).

of blowing up electricity sub-stations along the border) had petered-out (a bit like the electricity supply) the previous year. The time was ripe for a change of direction. Northern Ireland had ossified long enough. At Westminster, Labour leader Harold Wilson was on the cusp of a landmark general election victory over the jaded Tories, by now led by former hereditary peer Alec Douglas-Home; a kindly One Nation grandee who did his sums on an abacus. The omens looked to be in favour of change.

However, not to labour the point, Northern Ireland isn't Britain. A gust of fetid air has a habit of blowing in through an open window, confounding those arrogant enough to believe that history only moves in a linear direction. Faced with Unionist intransigence and growing calls for civil rights from the Catholic minority, O'Neill quickly found himself overwhelmed. In Belfast, Catholics were coming in for regular attack by loyalist gangs intent on burning them out of their homes. By 1968, events were spiralling out of control. Harold Wilson's Labour government of the day sent troops to Northern

Ireland to support the Stormont administration in restoring public order. Despite being initially welcomed by Catholics fearing loyalist mobs, the mood quickly soured and they became seen as an occupying army.

The hostility shown to the civil rights movement started to harden into more urgent demands for equality. Specifically, the protestors were drawing attention to the policy of internment without trial, introduced in 1971 to round up supposed IRA members. Out-of-date information and unreliable sources meant it was a spectacular disaster. Initially, 342 people were arrested and taken to makeshift camps – all of them Catholics or Republicans. Over the next forty-eight hours, seventeen people were killed, ten of them by the British Army in the Ballymurphy area of Belfast, including a Catholic priest and a mother of eight.

Outrage at the detention without trial saw more protests and confrontation. This culminated on 30 January 1972 in a march for civil rights in Derry. The authorities banned it (a tactic that had previously frustrated Daniel O'Connell's efforts), but it went ahead anyway. The particulars of what happened next are one of the more familiar tales for British audiences. Soldiers from the Parachute Regiment opened fire on marchers, shooting dead thirteen people (a fourteenth subsequently died of his injuries), while dozens more were injured. Here was Ireland's second 'Bloody Sunday'. This was the final straw. The presence of journalists and television cameras meant the world was given a front-row seat from which to witness Northern Ireland's carnage.

Eight weeks later, fifty years of devolved government at Stormont came to an end and the Parliament was prorogued; the inevitable conclusion to a sorry tale of misrule and incompetence which has blackened Britain's name around the world. Not only was Northern Ireland completely out of control, but the political class in Stormont was a fundamental part of the problem. If civil functions could not be discharged equitably, then Whitehall would have to run the place. After boarding the aeroplane at the end of his first visit to Northern Ireland, the story goes that Home Secretary Reginald Maudling remarked to his staff: 'For God's sake, bring me a large scotch. What a bloody awful country.'

⤙⤙

There's a wall in the Northern Ireland Office with photographs of the various secretaries of state in chronological order. It's a mosaic that tells the story of the British government's uneven efforts in dealing with Northern Ireland after the imposition of direct rule in March 1972 right the way through to the completion of the Good Friday Agreement settlement in 2010 and subsequent efforts to embed the process. It starts with Willie Whitelaw, that urbane old fixer on whom Margaret Thatcher would later rely so much. He took over as Stormont was being mothballed. His tenure was best remembered for a short-lived ceasefire and talks where leaders of the Provisional IRA were invited over to London for discussions.

The IRA's team included a young activist from Belfast and a former butcher's apprentice from Derry. It is quite a thought that Gerry Adams and Martin

McGuinness (for it was they) have been at the top table of Northern Ireland negotiations since the current Northern Ireland Secretary, James Brokenshire, was in kindergarten. Throughout the mayhem of the mid-1970s there were faltering efforts at dialogue and another brief ceasefire. But the instability and violence of the times meant that political efforts quickly foundered.

During the 1970s and 1980s, the figures that followed were often stern-looking types with military bearing. Men like Humphrey Atkins, Tom King and Patrick Mayhew fitted the part perfectly. Occasionally, someone more imaginative was appointed, like Jim Prior, or Peter Brook, but there was little political buy-in at the time to progress the dialogue they sought. The Kremlinology is instructive. From the 1970s to the 1990s, the Northern Ireland brief was a political backwater, with ministers expected to remain wedded to the grim status quo that Northern Ireland simply needed a sufficiently robust security response to bring it into line. Indeed, British government policy towards Northern Ireland from the early 1970s to the late 1980s met Einstein's classic definition of insanity: doing the same thing over and over again and expecting a different result. This approach summed up Roy Mason's tenure. He was appointed Northern Ireland Secretary by Labour Prime Minister James Callaghan between 1976 and 1979 and the legacy of this period is a grim litany of repressive measures and a casual disregard for legal due process and human rights. This was the era of the 'dirty war', where pretty much anything went. Torture of terrorist suspects, deployment of the SAS, jury-less trials and even the miasma of state agencies colluding with loyalist paramilitaries – all were sanctioned as part of the war against the Provisional IRA.

Northern Ireland had been an international PR disaster for the British government since the late 1960s and, under Mason, there was a concerted attempt to 'normalise' the situation. This meant the Royal Ulster Constabulary and Ulster Defence Regiment (the largest infantry in the British Army and, effectively, a local militia) assumed greater frontline roles in managing security. That both institutions were almost exclusively Protestant – the RUC was

90 per cent, the Ulster Defence Regiment 98 per cent – and merely locked in a 'them and us' mentality for the Catholic Nationalist minority was lost on Mason.

But his other legacy – the 'criminalisation' of paramilitary prisoners (denying them political status and treating them as ordinary criminals) – had even bigger repercussions. Republicans started by refusing to wear prison uniforms, wrapping themselves in prison blankets instead. This escalated into a 'dirty protest', whereby they refused to 'slop-out', instead spreading excrement over the walls in their cells. Yet, Mason and his securocrat agenda were unbending. It is a validation of how hardline his approach became that Margaret Thatcher continued it, leading, as it inexorably would, to the hunger strikes in 1981, in which ten Republican prisoners starved to death in protest. The propaganda victory became a potent recruiting sergeant for the Provisionals. So violence simply begot further violence and on it continued right through the 1980s and 1990s.

Eventually, however, politics broke through. In 1989, Peter Brook, an aristocratic, One Nation Tory, succeeded Douglas Hurd at the Northern Ireland Office. Brooke famously asserted that Britain had no 'selfish strategic or economic interest' in Northern Ireland and would accept unification if there was majority consent. 'It is not the aspiration to a sovereign, united Ireland against which we set our face, but its violent expression,' he added.

This approach, coupled with secret talks between John Hume, Leader of the constitutional nationalist Social Democratic and Labour Party (SDLP) and Sinn Féin President Gerry Adams, created the space for politics to take root and to eventually end the Provisional IRA's campaign and bring Republicans in from the cold. To be sure, it was a process that came in fits and starts, but the public recognition from the British government that it had no long-term special affinity in Northern Ireland remaining part of the British state was a powerful symbol that an elegant withdrawal, at a time unspecified somewhere down the road, was possible.

Events picked up pace during John Major's premiership, with an eventual IRA ceasefire in 1994 and the publication of a series of concordats with the Irish government that would later pave the way for 1998's Good Friday Agreement. Although things started badly. In 1991, the IRA launched an audacious bid to wipe out the British Cabinet. A van-mounted mortar was fired at Downing Street from across Whitehall. As the head of the Explosives Section of the Anti-Terrorist Branch, who defused one of the unexploded shells, explained in a (perhaps unintendedly) candid assessment:

> It was a remarkably good aim if you consider that the bomb was fired 250 yards [across Whitehall] with no direct line of sight. Technically, it was quite brilliant and I'm sure that many army crews, if given a similar task, would be very pleased to drop a bomb that close.[2]

Although significant political breakthroughs came on Major's watch, he was reliant on Ulster Unionists in the House of Commons to shore up his

---

2   Quoted in Peter Taylor's *Provos: The IRA and Sinn Fein* (London: Bloomsbury, 1998).

minority government, which was losing by-election after by-election as it imploded over Europe and the post-Thatcher agenda. After 1997, though, there was a shift in tempo. Enter Tony Blair. As Prime Minister, he and a succession of talented ministers took huge strides in building a political process that cemented the tentative peace accord. All of a sudden, the line-up on the wall in the Northern Ireland Office became a 'who's who' of many of New Labour's brightest stars: Mo Mowlam, Peter Mandelson, John Reid, Peter Hain and (my old boss) Shaun Woodward.

Blair, the arch-pragmatist, whose governing credo was 'what matters is what works', recognised the potential for a transformational breakthrough. He appointed Mo Mowlam as the first-ever female Northern Ireland Secretary. An earthy former academic anthropologist, Mowlam had been suffering from a brain tumour and as a result of her treatment had taken to wearing a wig. It is said she unnerved Unionists with her habit of removing it in meetings and calling everyone 'babe'. The prim and formal men of Ulster Unionism never warmed to her and, following the signing of the historic Good Friday Agreement in 1998, Mowlam was replaced by Peter Mandelson in a return to Cabinet after being forced to resign from the government a year earlier over the controversy generated by his non-disclosure of a personal mortgage. But Mandelson never 'got' Northern Ireland. The process listed on his watch as he struggled to grasp the issues and manage the personalities. Quintessentially a creature of British politics, he was a fish out of water.

Nevertheless, the space that the Good Friday Agreement opened up meant the watchtowers and razor wire could be pulled down. The soldiers disappeared from street corners and returned home. In a landmark review of policing, the former Chairman of the Conservative Party, Chris Patten, recommended the Royal Ulster Constabulary should be scrapped and rebuilt from the ground up as the more neutral-sounding 'Police Service of Northern Ireland', with targets to recruit a representative number of Catholics. Mason's 'criminals' were released on licence in their hundreds (a critical move to copper-fasten the process and one it is hard to imagine a Conservative government making). Blair's political deftness was the victory of politics, dialogue and persuasion over the brainless, unflinching militarism that had gone before. It represented a complete change of emphasis from trying to resolve 'the Irish Question' – the deepest thorn in the flesh of British politics – through state fiat. Of all the things Blair did or did not do in his decade as Prime Minister, the Northern Ireland peace and political process is one of the unsullied entries on his scorecard. 'The peace process' is the familiar shorthand for what was, in reality, two processes – yes, a peace process, where the gun could be removed from Northern Irish politics, but it was also a political process, whereby Northern Ireland's tribes can come together in a power-sharing administration and, hopefully, focus on more everyday concerns. The two are, even to this day, symbiotic. The promise of reconciling political objectives through exclusively peaceful methods holds the 'men of violence' in check, while the absence of conflict allows long-held material grievances to be addressed. Is it perfect? No. But politics is famously the art of the possible, not the perfect.

This, then, is a flavour of the weight of context for understanding why we are where we are in relation to Northern Ireland. British historical narrative doesn't really know how to include Ireland, so tries not to. This brief gallop through 800 years of British/English–Irish relations may seem unfamiliar. It probably jars, feels remote and doesn't fit with Britain's view of itself, then, or now. It's a frustrating legacy for contemporary ministers who are sent to make sense of Northern Ireland and its complex back story. Maudling's exasperation speaks for every minister who followed in his footsteps. However, the point of drawing attention to these events from Ireland's past is because they reverberate in the modern age. They help explain Irish suspicions about the trustworthiness of British statesmen, or Protestant worries about being sold out by the English. For most of us, they just pose awkward questions. Why would we raise a statue outside Parliament to an ethnic-cleansing mass murderer like Cromwell? Why would we stand by and allow more than a million Irish to starve to death, when their lands produced an abundance of food? Why would we send mercenaries like the 'Black and Tans' to kill and terrorise what were, in essence, British subjects? Why would we ignore the sectarianism of Unionist rule in Northern Ireland for fifty years? Why would we not instinctively side with the civil rights movement in the late 1960s, before we sent in the troops and allowed British soldiers to shoot fourteen of them dead on Bloody Sunday? Why? Why? Why?

CHAPTER TWO

BRITAIN'S JUST NOT THAT INTO NORTHERN IRELAND

I n many respects, the hardest question to answer in relation to Northern Ireland is also the simplest. Why is Northern Ireland still part of the United Kingdom? It is one of British politics' great puzzlements. A 94-year-old sticking-plaster solution to avoid a messy and violent ethno-national conflagration on the island of Ireland in the first two decades of the twentieth century has endured for, seemingly, no other reason than political inertia. Certainly not because the dispensation created in

1922 at the time of partition was a success. In fact, the creation of Northern Ireland is one of the worst decisions taken by any British government during the whole of the twentieth century (and certainly one of the most expensive), leading, as it did, first to the creation of a sectarian state that abused the position of a third of the population for half a century, before eventually metastasising into what euphemistically became known as 'the Troubles' and an incalculable loss of life and treasure up until recent times.

The endurance of Northern Ireland as an appendage to the United Kingdom ('of Great Britain *and* Northern Ireland') owes much to its marginal proximity. A province of just 1.8 million people (an equivalent population to the sleepy southern English county of Hampshire), it is in no meaningful way part of the UK at all. Geographical reality sees to that, with the torrents of the Irish Sea providing a permanent physical barrier from Britain. (Even at its narrowest point, from Belfast to Stranraer, the distance is around twenty miles – equivalent to that between Dover and Calais.)

It is, to an English audience, a far-away place of

which they know – are care – little. To be sure, the Scots, kissing cousins of Northern Ireland's original 'planter' Unionists (those lowland Scots Protestants sent to Ireland in the Cromwell era to create a loyal garrison population), may retain lingering affections for their brethren; but that sentiment no longer courses through the bloodstream of the vastly much more populous English – if, indeed, it ever did. And given immigration patterns from Ireland into the west of Scotland from the time of the famine, even Scotland is a house divided on the question of Ireland (with a quarter of the population having Irish ancestry). Writing here in England, Northern Ireland is seen as a strange little place, full of odd and violent people with whom the English have next to no affinity. Befuddlement, irritation and despair are more common emotions. We wonder why the IRA used to want to blow us up and why men in orange sashes and bowler hats want to march down streets where they are not wanted. If we think of them at all.

Northern Ireland is our unloved lodger. We are forced to cohabit because of some binding agreement, signed by our forefathers, from which there is seemingly no pain-free escape clause. However, the nature of our relationship is contractual rather than emotional; a dubious inheritance from a beleaguered interwar government facing the reality of making a messy concession in the face of a guerrilla war it could not win on one side and the emotional blackmail of Ulster loyalists on the other. It chose what it believed was the lesser of two evils, unable to manufacture an elegant withdrawal from Britain's first colony. So it split the difference, granting independence over most of the country to a Republican insurgency it could not supress, while creating a protectorate for loyalists it didn't love but felt it owed. For a state whose empire then covered two-thirds of the globe, it was a large, humiliating concession. The Easter Rising of 1916, a week-long insurrection by armed Republicans against British rule, began a process of events which, in time, would signify the beginning of the end of the British Empire, with countless other national liberation movements taking their lead from Ireland's example. So it's hardly surprising that a succession of governments paid little attention to the vestigial statelet of Northern Ireland, a painful reminder of a national humiliation.

In return, members of Northern Ireland's idiosyncratic political class were given *carte blanche* to run their affairs as they saw fit. In fact, the creation of Northern Ireland in 1922 was the most ambitious example of devolution ever allowed by the centralising twentieth-century British state. 'Metro mayors' may be all the rage across England at the moment, but for fifty years, Northern Ireland had its own Prime Minister. However, the crude majoritarianism built into the gerrymandered settlement was an open invitation for Unionists to act corruptly. So act corruptly they did, determinedly controlling the levers of power, removing political and economic agency from, as they regarded them, the numerically and religiously inferior Catholics. The spoils of the state were kept for the 'right' people: the 'loyal' Protestant Unionist people. There are innumerable books detailing the discrimination at the very heart of the Northern Irish state between partition in 1922 and the imposition of direct rule from Whitehall in 1972, save to say that these events are little discussed and poorly understood in British politics. (Not helped by the fact that British MPs were forbidden from tabling parliamentary questions about Northern Ireland, as its affairs were considered a devolved matter.)

Britain joined the Irish in their linguistic tradition of understatement, referring to the events that took place from 1968 until the late 1990s as 'the Troubles'. (Just as the Second World War was referred to in Ireland as 'The Emergency'.) We sought to minimise the horror of a secessionist uprising, with the fallout felt across many English cities and towns, reducing it to the status of 'a little local difficulty', like neighbours quarrelling over a privet hedge. A row that nevertheless saw the British Army's longest-ever campaign take place within the borders of its own country.

We should not be surprised at a particular type of British amnesia. When it comes to remembering our role in Irish affairs, there is much we would like to forget. When acclaimed British film director Ken Loach's Palme D'or-winning *The Wind That*

Shakes the Barley was released in 2006, it played on 300 screens across France, but just forty in the UK. The film depicts the activities of a 'flying column' of young IRA activists in County Cork during the 'War of Independence' against British rule, focusing on the eventual split between pragmatists and purists over the treaty signed with Britain that paved the way for the creation of the Irish Free State, but which also led to the partition of the country, fuelling the subsequent Irish Civil War of 1922–23.

To the Irish, the events of those tumultuous years are second nature. Michael Collins. The Black and Tans. De Valera. The War of Independence. Partition. But, to most people in this country, all this represents a secret history. It is not taught in our schools or depicted on our televisions. The Irish state broadcaster RTE commissioned a landmark period drama, *Rebellion*, about the Easter Rising in 1916, yet it did not air on British terrestrial television, despite the events being just as much part of the warp and weft of British history. If, indeed, there is a single difference between the Irish and the English, it comes down to understanding why the Brits are always cast as villains in Hollywood blockbusters. The English are puzzled and a little bit hurt at the constant depiction of their country-men as scoundrels and heartless murderers. On the receiving end of a litany of English misdeeds down the centuries, the Irish instinctively recognise why they are.

When Martin McGuinness first visited Down-ing Street to meet Prime Minister Tony Blair as a member of a Sinn Féin delegation, he was appar-ently shown into the Cabinet Room and remarked: 'So this is where the damage was done.' Blair's chief of staff, Jonathan Powell, the man who, more than any other single individual, negotiated and drove the Northern Irish peace process, assumed McGuin-ness was referring to the 1991 IRA mortar attack on John Major's Cabinet. McGuinness had to explain he meant the signing of the treaty back in 1922 that divided the island of Ireland. If the foundational events of the Irish Free State are little understood by the English, the same applies to 'the Troubles'. Again, memories of unwise and unjust political decisions mean there is little appetite for dwelling on the past. And there is much to forget. From the early 1970s and the imposition of direct rule from Whitehall, successive ministers sanctioned things that, forty years on, are rather embarrassing to be associated with. In more recent times, since the peace process began, we are used to our Prime Ministers playing the part of 'honest broker' rather than participant in the conflict, but this is a relatively new role.

State papers released in December 2015 under the thirty-year rule reveal that in 1985 Margaret Thatcher suggested to her Irish counterpart, Garret Fitzgerald, that the town of Dundalk, over the border in the Irish Republic, could be bombed in a bid to stymie fleeing Republicans who sought sanctuary there. The reports do not appear to capture Fitzgerald's reaction to this suggestion of state-sponsored terrorism, but Thatcher's mind set is instructive. It is of a piece with the 'securocrat' belief that a military solution was possible against the Provisional IRA. This was, regrettably, the default British government view throughout the 1970s and 1980s. Former Labour Northern Ireland Secretary Roy

Mason personified this dunder-headed machismo, remarking that he was going to squeeze the IRA 'like toothpaste' and bragged before Labour lost the 1979 election that 'the Provos' were 'weeks away' from defeat.

Other state papers published in 2014 revealed a plan cooked up by the Northern Ireland Office to redraw the boundary between Northern Ireland and the Republic, laying out a series of options which included ceding most of heavily Catholic Derry to the Irish Republic and, potentially, handing over West Belfast. This was to be achieved by turning it into a 'walled ghetto'. In a wonderful piece of understatement, the *Irish Independent* reported: '...officials later noted that while moving half-a-million people – mostly Catholics – might be acceptable for a totalitarian regime, human rights arguments would be an obstacle'.

In a not-too-subtle bid to get unwanted Catholics out of a freshly carved Northern Ireland, it was suggested there could be loyalty tests in order to claim benefits, while 'large-scale' internment was also suggested as a means to help 'drive out large numbers'. Stories like this are easy to dismiss as eccentric kite-flying, but when they are remarks made by the Prime Minister of the country, or proposals drawn up by her officials and put before her, they are automatically given a chilling validity. These crazy suggestions – and others which have not yet seen the light of day – reveal how extreme official thinking actually became. Indisputably, Margaret Thatcher had a jaundiced view of the Irish. Perhaps Peter Mandelson's vignette about meeting her soon after he was appointed Northern Ireland Secretary in 1999 sheds some light:

> She came up to me and she said, 'I've got one thing to say to you, my boy.' She said, 'You can't trust the Irish, they're all liars,' she said. 'Liars, and that's what you have to remember, so just don't forget it.'
>
> With that she waltzed off and that was my only personal exposure to her.[3]

---

3   Quoted in *Irish Times*, 18 April 2013.

This is of a piece with what we know to be her attitude to Northern Ireland and Irish affairs more broadly; mistrustful, simplistic and, well, bigoted. In 2001, it came to light that Thatcher had suggested to a senior diplomat who was negotiating with the Irish government over the landmark Anglo-Irish Agreement in 1985 that Catholics living in Northern Ireland could be moved to live in southern Ireland instead. She made the suggestion to Sir David Goodall during a late-night conversation at Chequers. He explained:

> She said, 'If the northern [Catholic] population want to be in the south, well why don't they move over there? After all, there was a big movement of population in Ireland, wasn't there?'
>
> Nobody could think what it was. So finally I said, 'Are you talking about Cromwell, Prime Minister?' She said, 'That's right, Cromwell.'[4]

So what shaped Thatcher's dislike of the Irish? Was it

---

4   Quoted in *Belfast Telegraph*, 15 April 2013.

the loss of her close colleagues, MPs Airey Neave and Ian Gow, in Republican bombings, or her own near-miss at the hands of the IRA in Brighton in 1984, when they detonated a bomb in the Grand Hotel during the Conservative Party conference? Or was it simply that a Grantham girl remembered Cromwell fondly? (Perhaps because his first successful battle of the English Civil War was to capture the town from Crown forces?)

With so little regard for the Irish, it is perhaps no wonder that Britain's record during those dark years of the 1970s, 1980s and 1990s was a catalogue of controversial counter-insurgency measures that were first used to quell insurrections in places like Aden and Kenya, upheld by a belief that if you treat the natives firmly enough, they will eventually toe the line. There is much that to contemporary eyes is simply astounding. Not to mention reeking of double standards. Indeed, if you think Guantanamo Bay has been an affront to legal due process, try internment without trial, introduced in Northern Ireland in 1971 with hundreds of innocent men (all of them Catholics or Republicans) dragged from their homes and jailed for months without charge. Think Iraq's notorious Abu Ghraib prison was appalling? Clearly you have never heard of Castlereagh detention centre and the torture programme carried out behind its walls by agents of the British state on what were, when all was said and done, British citizens.

Then there's the 'hooded men' case, where, in 1971, fourteen ordinary Catholic men were rounded up and subjected to 'deep interrogation' techniques, which included hooding, being forced into stress positions for long periods, exposed to white noise and deprived of sleep, food and water. In 1978, the European Court of Human Rights judged their treatment was inhuman and degrading, but stopped short of calling these infamous 'five techniques' torture. (The Bush administration later used that ruling as the legal basis for its own interrogation programme in Iraq and Afghanistan.)

While the 'Ballymurphy Ten' were civilians gunned down by the British Army during the implementation of internment and a few weeks before the better-known 'Bloody Sunday' atrocity occurred. A Catholic priest tending to a wounded man and a mother of eight were among those shot dead in the street. Like Bloody Sunday (when fourteen civil rights marchers were killed in 1972), soldiers from the Parachute Regiment were responsible.

Think shoot-to-kill is rough justice when applied to Jihadi terrorists with guns? Well, it was an approach used against the civilian Catholic population in Northern Ireland – not just the IRA (upon whom it was unquestionably used) – in the early 1970s as the army's shadowy Military Reaction Force ran amok. These were plain-clothed soldiers operating, in the estimation of one of their number, as a 'death squad', shooting at indiscriminate targets from cars in drive-by killings, with no other purpose, it seems, than to induce terror. Conveniently, records of their activities have since been destroyed.

Not to overlook the really murky stuff.

Like the 'dirty war' counter-insurgency effort handled by the British Army's anodyne-sounding Force Research Unit, which ran agents and targeted Republicans for assassination, including Gerry Adams and Martin McGuinness. This included figures like Brian Nelson, who, while working as a British agent, was also a high-ranking member of the loyalist Ulster Defence Association and was personally implicated in twenty-six murders, including one of the most notorious – that of Catholic solicitor Pat Finucane in 1989, who was shot at point-blank range fourteen times while his wife and children looked on in horror at the kitchen table of their Belfast home.

Then there was 'Agent Stakeknife' – alleged to be IRA hard man Freddie Scappaticci – the highest-ranking agent the British had in the Provisional IRA, responsible for their internal security unit, which interrogated, tortured and killed informers (including other British assets). It is suggested Scappaticci is responsible for up to fifty murders.

These are just some of the 'known knowns' in terms of what we definitely know was sanctioned by successive British governments against – let us not forget – their own people within the borders of the British state. Actions carried out in our name. These events are little understood on this side of the Irish Sea, but if they had taken place on the streets of London, what would we think? Would we let the army get away with shooting demonstrators in Trafalgar Square? Would we allow the police to round up people with no charge before subjecting them to deep interrogation? How would we react if vicars and pregnant women were killed in the street by our own soldiers?

Furthermore, it begs the question: if this is what we know happened, with no one seriously disputing that the above events took place in the ways described, just how bad are the 'known unknowns'? The events that took place during the Troubles that have still to come to light? Would some sort of truth and reconciliation process, of the kind frequently talked about in Northern Ireland in a bid to heal wounds and 'deal with the past', reveal, for instance, that British agents inside Republican paramilitaries deliberately targeted civilians in some of their infamous bombings in order to discredit them? After all, the level of British infiltration was such that it is claimed a quarter of Provisional IRA members were working for British state security agencies, rising to half of the organisation's senior management.

The point about collusion, whether in connection to Patrick Finucane's assassination, or in any
of the dozens of other cases that we know about, is
that it makes Britain culpable in state-sanctioned
murder. It instantly reduces the British state to a
participant in the conflict, something successive
governments have been loath to concede. It seeps
into the grain of Britain's international reputation,
leaving an indelible, bloody stain. We tumble off
the moral high ground and, in turn, validate the
actions of Republican paramilitaries who, throughout the Troubles, always posited they were 'at war'
with Britain. Collusion is a powerful leveller that
reduces Britain to the status of a South American
junta or African dictatorship. Places where governments torture and murder their political opponents.

But collusion is not only about conspiracy to
commit murder with proxy paramilitaries, it's also
about creating a culture of impunity where the
truth is actively covered up. This was brought to
light by the Police Ombudsman for Northern Ireland's report into the 1994 Loughinisland massacre,
where loyalists opened fire in a crowded rural bar,

killing six patrons and wounding five. The initial investigation into the murders was characterised by 'incompetence, indifference and neglect'.[5] Although the police knew the suspects' names within twenty-four hours of the shooting, they deliberately delayed making arrests. Neither did they investigate allegations that an RUC officer warned suspects that they were to be arrested – and that one initial suspect was in fact an RUC informant. The Ombudsman, Dr Michael Maguire, found that police records had been destroyed and the getaway car driven by the gunmen had been contaminated.

Is this evidence merely of police bungling, or even just a case of overstretched officers punch-drunk from investigating the litany of killings during the Troubles? The Ombudsman's assessment bears quoting:

There has been considerable debate in academic publications, reports by nongovernmental

---

5   'The Murders at the Heights Bar, Loughinisland, 18 June 1994',
     Police Ombudsman for Northern Ireland, p. 4.

agencies and in the various inquiries into allegations of State related killings in Northern
Ireland. No consensus has emerged as to what
it actually means. I am of the view that individual examples of neglect, incompetence and/or
investigative failure are not (de facto) evidence
of collusion.

However, a consistent pattern of investigative
failures may be considered as evidence of collusion depending on the context and specifics
of each case. This is particularly the case when
dealing with police informants, who were participating in crime.[6]

In other words, 'collusion' is not just active part-
icipation with loyalist paramilitaries, but also the
connivance to cover up the truth, by, in this case,
frustrating the investigation by warning suspects
and destroying and tainting evidence. Summing
up the catalogue of malfeasance by the RUC in
1994, the Ombudsman said he had 'no hesitation

---

6   Ibid., p. 6.

in unambiguously determining that collusion is a significant feature of the Loughinisland murders'.[7]

Again, what right have we to upbraid the world's less savoury regimes for the treatment of their people, telling them to remove the mote from their eye, while we continue to have a plank sticking out of ours?

What was the view of collusion from within Whitehall? How did the conversations go? 'Minister, can we have clearance to defeat the Provisional IRA by siding with loyalists and getting them to do our dirty work?' Perhaps it wasn't quite that stark. Given the civil service's love of euphemisms, did mandarins and securocrats talk about 'neutralising' their opponents? Or 'seeking a conclusive victory, using whatever methods are deemed sufficient'? There will certainly have been talk about not 'handing a propaganda victory' to the IRA by charging British soldiers, spies and officials who sanctioned, planned, implemented and covered up acts of collusion with paramilitaries. Perhaps the still-classified state papers of the 1970s and 1980s, which approved

7   Ibid., p. 7.

the dirty war against the IRA and then turned a blind eye to its inevitable consequences, capture more than bureaucratic indifference to this moral squalor. Hopefully, there were other voices in the discussion, pleading to stop and think of the consequences.

However, it's unlikely we will ever be given the chance to find out. There is little appetite for raking over the coals of Northern Ireland's bloody history from any of its parties, but there is none, whatsoever, from Whitehall. There is little to no prospect of an international body hearing former paramilitaries, soldiers and spies state baldly what they did during the three decades of bloody internecine conflict. We will continue to hear talk of dealing with the past but there will be no 'Oprah-fication' of Northern Ireland's Troubles, with all its messiness poured forth for the purposes of communal 'sharing'. We want to forget about the place.

The British government simply has too much to lose from the truth emerging, especially if it washes up at the doors of former ministers and politicians. Nearly 3,600 people were killed during the period and countless more were maimed, but there is little

common ground about how and what is commemorated, remembered or conveniently forgotten. And,
crucially, who is brought to book, either legally or
in moral terms, for the deaths and atrocities that
occurred. Of course, no one will publicly disown the
idea of some sort of truth and reconciliation process,
but everyone has something unpleasant to answer
for. The real blocker on a deal in establishing such
a process, however, is the British government itself.

Before we can ever get to that point, we first require
some long-overdue honesty from the British political class. There is plainly no interest in remaining
in Northern Ireland, whose place in the Union is
attached by nothing more adhesive than conven-
tion these days. Would our Westminster politicians
cancel their holidays to trudge the highways and
byways of West Belfast or North Antrim, making the
case for people there to remain part of the UK if a
referendum on its constitutional status ever came
to pass?

A few dewy-eyed Unionist ultras aside, it seems highly unlikely. Yet, they were entirely willing to do so when it was Scotland on the table. Campaigners from all sides of British politics were happy to do whatever was needed in order to avert a Scottish breakaway. There were historical and emotional connections that were thought to be worth preserving, not least the complex economic and administrative ties that bind Scotland to England. There is no similar affinity discernible in relation to Northern Ireland. And, given the province is reliant on British handouts, there is no net economic impact to it leaving the UK. Dealing with the aftermath of a vote to leave the UK and join the Irish Republic is a simple case of 'lifting and shifting' sovereignty, with little effect felt on the rest of the UK.

So why have successive governments not moved to do so? There was clearly reticence for a long time because of the terrible price paid by so many Northern Irish families during the Great War. The Unionist blood spilt as the 36th Ulster Division was mowed down at the Somme in 1916 was a potent, visceral reminder to British politicians of Unionists' sacrifice. The message was clear: Britain owed them a metaphorical and literal blood debt. But the First World War is now consigned to historical memory. Put bluntly, there is no one left alive in Northern Ireland who suffered the privations of the First World War who can yell 'traitor' with any moral purchase at backsliding British politicians. Moreover, our understanding of those years has now evolved, with far more appreciation now (rightly) paid to the tens of thousands of Catholics from southern Ireland who fought in the British Army as well, on the basis that defending the rights of small nations would include action to finally free Ireland from Britain's grasp.

So we treat Northern Ireland as some other place because that's precisely how we regard it. Perhaps one single measure, more than anything else, summarises this. The use of baton rounds and water cannons to quell civil disturbances has become a regular feature of the policing and security response in Northern Ireland. Yet they remain unused in Britain. In fact, the thought of their use in any British city, or against, say, student demonstrators, would be utterly unthinkable. When he was Mayor of London, Boris Johnson rashly purchased two second-hand water cannons following the London riots of 2011, but was publicly slapped down by then Home Secretary Theresa May, who flatly refused him licences to deploy them.

But, in most of the media coverage of the various disputes in Northern Ireland, their regular usage merits little more than a passing remark. In fact, they are invariably – and incorrectly – described as 'non-lethal'. Yet history proves otherwise. The University of Ulster found that the use of such 'non-lethal' weapons in policing the Troubles led to the deaths of seventeen people, ten of whom were aged eighteen or under. We have acquiesced when it comes to tolerating such barbaric practices because we regard the Northern Irish as a place apart, where it is permissible to employ quasi-military tactics against civilians with a casualness that would have British MPs screaming at ministers if used anywhere else. That we have normalised these brutal practices against civilians, whatever their cause, within a corner of the British state, is an appalling, dehumanising relic.

The otherness with which Britain regards Northern Ireland is, in fact, long-established government
policy, ever since Peter Brooke's speech which
repositioned Britain as an honest broker, rejecting
territorial chauvinism and instead upholding 'the
principle of consent'. This has been the position
ever since. As long as the majority of people want to
remain part of Britain, this wish will be honoured.
Of course, this is hardly a ringing endorsement of
the status quo. No one in British politics seems
to care about making the case that Northern Ireland *should* remain part of the UK, as they are
more than happy to do with Scotland or Wales.
Of course, the prospect of the Welsh opting for full-
blown independence is so remote as to be purely
academic. (Indeed, the referendum on the creation
of the Welsh Assembly was passed by the slen-
derest of margins back in 1998 – 50.3 per cent to
49.7 per cent. If a few thousand votes had gone the
other way, Wales would still be run from Whitehall.) Yet, if there was a sudden surge in Nationalist
sentiment sometime in the future, it is hard to imagine the rest of the UK being overly perturbed.

Wales – without oil and nuclear submarine bases – is simply of less strategic importance to the UK than Scotland. But, unlike Northern Ireland, Wales is tightly bound into the British state (if for no other reason than because it shares a long land border with England) and it is still effectively run, assembly aside, as a region of England.

Northern Ireland is in a category of its own. Indeed, nowhere else does Britain effectively share sovereignty with another state as it does with the Republic of Ireland over Northern Ireland, from the time of the Anglo-Irish Agreement back in 1985 onwards. There is no similar arrangement with the Spanish over Gibraltar, or with Argentina over the Falklands. The Good Friday Agreement effectively placed Northern Ireland in an antechamber. If there is a majority that opts for Irish unity at some stage, then change will take place. No one is making a first-principles argument for Northern Ireland to remain part of the UK come what may. Indeed, nowhere else in British politics are our political leaders so flexible when it comes to our territorial sovereignty. Where Scotland is seen to be an opportunity worth holding on to, Northern Ireland is quietly regarded as a problem eventually worth jettisoning.

Scottish and Welsh elites in politics, business and culture are deeply integrated into British public life. In contrast, Northern Ireland's idiosyncratic political class finds few soulmates in Westminster. Unionist politicians – famously more British than the British – are now oddities in our political system. When former Northern Ireland First Minister Peter Robinson defended an evangelical Christian pastor, James McConnell, over the latter's description of Islam as a 'heathen' and 'satanic' religion, it is easy for Unionist politicians to seem like something from a different planet. Not to mention the double standard. If Robinson had been a minister, a frontbencher or leader of a council in Britain, and allied himself with such blatant Islamophobia, then he would have been out on his ear.

All of which reflects the essential fact that the British and Ulster Unionist sensibilities are firmly on different tracks. The only reason Northern Ireland's status is not more openly questioned is down to the sheer relief that the Troubles are over. Surely Unionists can see that one day this will not be enough? Although the Irish state renounced its territorial claims to Northern Ireland, previously written into its constitution and conceded as part of the Good Friday Agreement, its status will remain contested.

Democratic agitation, rather than armed struggle, will now continue to gnaw at the fraying ropes holding Northern Ireland in the Union. This is set in the context of British–Irish relations having steadily improved over recent decades. (There was even initial talk of the Queen participating in Irish state commemorations of the 1916 Easter Rising against British rule.) Indeed, in her state visit to Ireland back in 2011, Her Majesty laid a wreath to the IRA volunteers who fought against Britain in Ireland's War of Independence (to be sure, many had fought *for* Britain during the First World War). The prospect of 'Dublin rule' is no longer, plausibly, a spectre for Unionists. Not when even the Queen herself can bow in tribute at the memory of dead IRA men and women.

This growing amity between Britain and Ireland perversely makes Irish reunification more, not less, likely. The lack of belligerence from either side in contemporary Anglo-Irish relations provides a fulcrum upon which continued debate about the relationship between these isles can mature. Indeed, it is said to be a personal sadness to the Queen that it has taken so long for things to have reached this point. The threat to Unionist identity is diminished when it is abundantly clear these islands will cooperate more closely than ever before in the years and decades ahead.

Things are changing in the north too. While the 'sectarian headcount' may be a crude measure of political allegiance, it is worth noting that Catholics now outnumber Protestants at every level of Northern Ireland's education system. (Tellingly, this is true in the former Unionist citadels of Belfast and Derry.) Northern Ireland's in-built Protestant Unionist majority is shrinking; while the integrative logic of an all-Ireland offering to the outside world, increasingly important in terms of investment and tourism, seems to make the gerrymandered border an anachronism. In time, a similar referendum to the one we saw in Scotland will come to pass in Northern Ireland. When it arrives, it will be hard to imagine the English people and the British political class busting a gut to maintain the status quo.

Unionists need to accept this basic political reality and mentally and emotionally prepare themselves for its inevitable consequences. Although the Good Friday Agreement copper-fastens the principle of consent, Unionists should have read the small print. The other way of viewing this safeguard is that Northern Ireland is the only part of UK with a constitutional guarantee that a transfer of sovereignty *can* take place when the majority wishes it.

There are two distinct political choices in the years ahead. The first sees us maintain the fiction that Britain wants to retain Northern Ireland and that this constitutional arrangement is fit for purpose and represents the settled, unflinching final will of the people of Northern Ireland. This view would, logically, see Northern Ireland more thoroughly subsumed into the British state. Yet integration is precisely what Northern Ireland's political

elite – Nationalist and Unionist alike – *don't* want.
Clearly, Republicans and Nationalists hate the idea
of having their identity diminished by becoming
more British, but there are downsides for Unionists too. It would see, for instance, abortion laws
extended to Northern Ireland (currently the only
place in the UK not covered by the 1967 Abortion
Act). Strident opposition to abortion is one of the
few issues that generates a united front from most
Nationalists and Unionists.

What Nationalists want is to develop sinews
with the south in a bid to 'Irishise' the province.
This stretches from demands for Gaelic road signs
through to cross-border development bodies.
Unionists simply want maximum local autonomy
and freedom to manage their own affairs *sans*
power-sharing with Catholic Nationalists, if they
could get away with it. They astutely recognise their
particular traditions, the Orange marches and
instinctive social conservatism, are now seriously
out of step with the British mainstream. (Indeed,
an illustration of this is the row between the Irish
Presbyterian Church (96 per cent of whose members

live in Northern Ireland) and the Scottish Presbyterians over the latter's softer line on the acceptance of same-sex marriage, causing the former to boycott sessions of the church's General Assembly for two years in a row.)

The second big choice about Northern Ireland's future would see all parties – the British, the Northern Irish and the southern Irish – facing up to the glaring reality that partition of the island of Ireland is archaic. A historical compromise born of the fear of something worse that has simply lost its sting over recent years. Between 1922 and the collapse of Stormont in 1972, the default British position was one of complete indifference. After that, it was one of belligerence in the face of the Provisional IRA's campaign. Ministerial chest-puffing during this period crowded out any critical thinking about what was in the long-term best interests of the British people. (Ironically, the Provisional IRA's long campaign did much to prop up this intellectual *ancien regime*.) Now, with the situation transformed by twenty years of incremental political progress, there is little excuse for further inaction. So Northern Ireland finds itself in a period of flux, brought about by the possibilities of 'normal' politics. For much of the first nine decades of its existence, little has changed. Protestant Unionist privilege had been locked into the essence of the place with the threat of Republican violence pitted, by extension, against the British state. Now things are changed, changed utterly.

This will have the effect of accelerating trends that are already apparent. The stabilisation of politics within Northern Ireland will, in turn, serve to strengthen cooperation with the Irish Republic. The integrative forces – economic and demographic among them – will force a re-examination of its constitutional status. British politicians will be quite delighted if it does. Especially at the prospect of long-term savings. The £9 billion a year the British Exchequer pumps into Northern Ireland is equivalent to £170 million a day. If Northern Ireland was no longer on Britain's balance sheet it is unlikely that austerity would be biting anywhere near as hard for ordinary Britons. An unfair comparison? Not when Northern Ireland is increasingly viewed as a quixotic choice and one, given the option, we may wish to change our mind about.

After all, as already discussed, we show no sign we want the place.

The simple truth is that a lack of imagination among the British political elite is the only thing now holding up the chain of events that will see Northern Ireland leave the UK and become part of a new, single, integrated Irish state. In the decade or so to come, a combination of economics, demographics, the success of power-sharing in blunting harsh memories and breaking down animosities, and changes to the British state, particularly the impact of English devolution and the potential loss of Scotland, will make Irish unity look like the inevitable, logical end point of the fractured, bloody history of these isles.

So the question for British politics is simple: would it not be better to start preparing for that day?

CHAPTER THREE

SHEER MAGNETISM: HOW ECONOMIC INTEGRATION MAKES A SINGLE IRELAND INEVITABLE

A quiet revolution is taking place in north-west England. The conurbation of Greater Manchester is wresting control of much of its own economic policy-making, as part of the current government's 'Northern Powerhouse' initiative, designed to devolve sovereignty across a range of policy areas in order to allow local political leaders to find local solutions to help boost growth and productivity.

The new metro mayor for Greater Manchester, set to be directly elected in May 2017, will also inherit control of the £6 billion NHS and social care budget for the area. With a population of 2.8 million, Greater Manchester is nearly as big as Wales and with its clearly defined territorial autonomy and bespoke governance arrangements it will become, in effect, the fifth nation of the United Kingdom.

Perhaps what's most amazing is that the Greater Manchester devolution deal has been delivered with a few strokes of a Treasury mandarin's pen. There is no great fuss about this radical redrawing of the administrative arrangements for England's second city. There has been no drawn-out process, just a meeting of minds between local officials and political leaders, who have proven their mettle with successful regeneration schemes over recent decades (inspired in no small part by regenerating the city centre after the devastating IRA bombing in 1996), and a UK Treasury that realises, belatedly, that it cannot run the whole UK economy on a single engine, with London overheating and other provincial centres operating at half-power.

With a much smaller population and less complex economy, a transfer of Northern Ireland's sovereignty is, if anything, even more straightforward. Bluntly, it is smaller (at around £37 billion, the value of Northern Ireland's economy is just two-thirds that of Greater Manchester's on £56 billion) and of less strategic importance (which is the polite way of saying there is less of it to get wrong). Of course, what is not straightforward is arriving at the point where that transfer is a regarded as a done deal. The politics has to draw level with the economics.

Economics, however, is the focus of this chapter and it's important to recognise that what's happening in Greater Manchester is also taking place in the West Midlands, Merseyside and South Yorkshire, as the provinces of England undergo the biggest bout of devolution since the Second World War in a bid to reenergise their local economies with a much-needed infusion of power and finance. The added piquancy is that all this comes courtesy of a Conservative government, determined to place politics at the service of economics in a bid to address the deep-rooted problems affecting these areas.

The whole point of the city-region model is that it takes account of real-world economic geography. Places with clearly defined economic potential. A spatial model that embraces local supply chains, travel to work areas and clusters of feeder towns. In other words, a pragmatic, enlightened view of what makes a place a place, unencumbered by artificial constructs and arbitrary borders. Everything, in other words, Northern Ireland is not.

What should Northern Ireland make of this? With a much smaller population, an engorged public sector, fiscal deficit and high, structural poverty and worklessness, it should realise that it too is ripe for reform. Take one illustration. The Northern Ireland Executive employs around 27,000 civil servants managing the affairs of 1.8 million people, while the European Commission has 33,000 officials dealing with the EU's 743 million people.

A report by the Northern Ireland Statistics and Research Agency (NISRA) on the 'Structure of the NI Economy', published in December 2015, highlights how peripheral Northern Ireland's economy is to the UK as a whole. The analysis – the latest available – covers 2012 and compares the GDP of Northern Ireland, Scotland and the UK as a whole. The figures are stark. Northern Ireland's economy was worth just £37.2 billion (roughly equivalent to the size of Yemen's), compared to £129 billion for Scotland and £1.6 trillion for the UK as a whole. Even accounting for the size differentials, this is marginal. So although Northern Ireland makes up 2.8 per cent of the UK's total population, it comprises just 2.2 per cent of its overall economy.

GDP per head was £20,409, compared to Scotland's £24,317 and £25,985 for the UK as a whole. While Scotland's was 94 per cent of the UK average, Northern Ireland's was just 79 per cent. Unsurprisingly, Northern Ireland's labour market also lags behind UK averages in many key regards. Although the rate of economic inactivity (26.3 per cent) is at its lowest since records began, it remains much higher than the UK average (21.7 per cent). What higher-value employment there is relies heavily on the public sector (although, admittedly, this share is falling due to Westminster-inspired cuts). Perhaps most alarmingly though, Northern Ireland's private service sector output has declined by 8.2 per cent from the peak recorded in the fourth quarter of 2006, according to NISRA's quarterly 'Index of Services', while the UK reported an increase of 16.3 per cent over the same period.

There are two fairly obvious conclusions. The first is that Northern Ireland is the least valuable, dynamic and diverse part of the UK economy. Second, it is plain enough that the economic dividend of peace and political process has not been felt keenly enough. Clearly, thirty years of the Troubles hardly helped matters, but Northern Ireland's economic woes are deep-seated. Agriculture and declining manufacturing industries make up too large a part of the economy, as does the public sector.

Regardless of whether Irish unity is viewed as a panacea for Northern Ireland's problems (it isn't), there has been remarkably little serious consideration about how the two parts of the island of Ireland could work together more harmoniously – improving their productive capacity and spreading prosperity – if they were part of a single state, with the strategies and assets of both parts of the island pointing in the same direction for maximum effect. Theoretically, the benefits are clear: the border is an artificial division and the respective populations are small enough and complementary enough to make uniting their economic efforts a common-sense solution. At present, Northern Ireland and the Republic are the only dinner guests positioned at opposite ends of a banqueting table.

Indeed, a major study published in November 2015 makes the case that Irish unity brings with it massive economic wins for both parts of the island of Ireland. 'Modelling Irish Unification' is the work of a respected team of academics led by Dr Kurt Hübner, director of the Institute for European Studies at the University of British Columbia. The researchers modelled various scenarios, including the effects of fiscal harmonisation, the reduction of trade barriers, transportation costs and currency transactions, narrowing the productivity gap between Northern Ireland and the more productive south, the impact of joining the euro and the effects of fiscal transfers from the British state in plugging Northern Ireland's budgetary black hole. (Tellingly, it is the first such simulation of economic and political integration, which, given Northern Ireland's hotly disputed status, seems extraordinary.)

The results show that 'political and economic unification of the North and South would likely result in a sizable boost in economic output and incomes in the North and a smaller boost in the ROI'.[8] The report calculates that integrating Northern and southern Ireland could drive out value equivalent to €36 billion during the first eight years, and while the Republic would see a more modest, but still considerable boost, the biggest effect would be to 'encourage[s] foreign capital inflows into Northern Ireland'.[9] The report argues that '"borders matter" to a much greater degree than most observers would expect'.[10] And while the economies of both jurisdictions are interlinked and interdependent, they are not aligned, 'differ[ing] enormously in

---

8   Quoted in 'Modelling Irish Unification', KLC Consulting, August 2015.
9   Ibid.
10 Ibid.

terms of structure, output and growth'.[11] The authors characterise the current differences between the Irish Republic and Northern Ireland. The former is 'a strongly outward-looking and export-intensive economy ... its long-term excellent growth record very much is based on a globally competitive regime of foreign direct investment'. The latter is 'a relatively more inward-looking economy that shares features of an economic periphery inside the UK'.[12] This results in GVA per capita being 159 per cent higher in the south and although both jurisdictions have recovered from the 2008–09 downturn, Northern Ireland again lags behind.

The Irish Republic's record in recent years – a highly competitive tax regime and a relentless focus on winning foreign direct investment – has 'earned the ROI the highest level of trade-openness among G20 nations'. Moreover, it is 'this kind of policy framework that can be anticipated in NI if it unifies with the ROI and becomes integrated into the island economy'.[13]

---

11   Ibid.
12   Ibid.
13   Ibid.

The research team modelled a series of propositions in ascending order of optimism. They began by assuming that a unified Irish state picks up the costs of absorbing the bill for Northern Ireland from day one, as well as de-duplicating functions – but that adopting the Republic's tax regime and foreign investment policy platform has no immediate effect. Even in this pessimistic forecast, GDP across the island of Ireland increases by €15.8 billion by 2025, a 3.1 per cent increase in GDP across the whole island. In their second assessment, they again assume the Republic picks up Northern Ireland's bill, but that this time Northern Ireland benefits from inward investment. The all-island effect on GDP accumulates to €31.2 billion by 2025. The least pessimistic assessment again sees the south inherit the north's debts while reducing duplicated public expenditure by 2 per cent a year, but this scenario realises the proper potential from foreign direct investment. This time, the accumulated gain for the newly integrated island of Ireland is €35.6 billion by 2025, with the benefits heavily weighted in Northern Ireland's favour by a two-to-one margin.

What the modelling shows is that the more thought-out and planned-through the scenario, the better the outcome. So, if there is early work to scope out how Northern Ireland can emulate the Irish Republic, in terms of positioning itself to maximise its effectiveness in winning foreign direct investment, it will have a bigger and earlier effect on GDP. This may seem fairly obvious, but there has been little in the way of serious analysis of the economic effects of Irish reunification and precious little planning, and this report provides a serious benchmark for future work. It adds empirical weight to intuitive common sense: that both jurisdictions in the island of Ireland would be better off integrating their economic efforts for the benefit of all the people of the island of Ireland.

If not a panacea for Northern Ireland's economic ailments, Dr Hübner's research does present a rigorous, plausible, practical and workable way forward. How does Unionism, wedded to a plainly failing status quo, answer the charge that Irish reunification makes eminent economic good sense? Indeed, what the report shows is that hard-headed realism now belongs to those advocating a united Ireland, with Unionists reduced to denying economic reality and clinging to an out-moded, faith-based romanticism about the province's economic prospects. This 'revisionist' narrative about Ireland's economic future – both parts of it – should now be the basis for intelligent discussion. And not a minute too soon. The consequences of Britain's exit from the European Union are uncertain enough, but what is guaranteed is that Northern Ireland will suffer more than anywhere else in the UK. As a drag anchor on the rest of us, there should now be renewed interest in British politics about how to accommodate a long-term solution, to safeguard the prosperity of the people of Northern Ireland.

What about the Republic? Opinion here may well blanch at the immediate prospect of picking up the tab for Northern Ireland, an assumed factor in Dr Hübner's report; however, there is a sliding scale of arrangements that could be put in place to taper the effects of unifying the two jurisdictions. Indeed, the report looks at the issue of political unification and its effect on the economy, and the authors argue that their modelling 'assumes no political frictions or political transition costs'. This is not remiss as such costs are not necessarily negative, 'particularly in the case where economic unification is a democratically legitimised event'.[14] (Again, the politics of Irish unity need to catch up with the economics.)

Thus, southern fears of being 'lumbered' with the north are unfounded. As are Unionist claims (and those of middle-class Catholics working in comfortable public sector occupations) that the Republic cannot afford to take responsibility for Northern Ireland. The report makes clear that unity presents net benefits for both jurisdictions. This is before we factor in handover arrangements that would see, for example, Northern Ireland still able to access EU regeneration aid and farming subsidies (which will be lost when Britain leaves the EU, despite watery assurances from the UK Treasury about underwriting the costs in the short term). It would also be likely that Britain would agree to a period of harmonisation during any transfer of sovereignty

---

14   Ibid.

and make reasonable arrangements for any legacy commitments like public sector pensions. After all, Ireland is one of the UK's main export markets and a successful integration of Northern and southern Ireland is in Britain's economic self-interest too.

One of the key aspects of economic integration between both jurisdictions is creating the same fiscal framework. This is surprisingly uncontentious in Northern Ireland. Indeed, it is already in prospect, with the Executive proposing to harmonise corporation tax levels with the Irish Republic from 2018. Former First Minister Peter Robinson, the leading proponent of the move, described winning permission from Whitehall to proceed with the plan as 'one of the achievements of the past few years that I am most proud of'.[15] It was a prize that came after a great deal of lobbying, with the last Labour government refusing the request (worried about increasing Northern Ireland's fiscal deficit with the UK Treasury), before David Cameron relented. The hope in Northern Ireland is that they will be better able to

---

15   Quoted in the *Financial Times*, 23 November 2015.

compete for foreign direct investment with the Irish Republic, which has enjoyed a corporation tax rate of just 12.5 per cent since 2003. Historically, Ireland has sought to make its economy more competitive through keeping business taxes low, culminating in the 12.5 per cent rate, much to the chagrin of other EU member states, who have criticised its aggressive taxation regime, allowing it to cream off the spoils of international investment.

But tiny Ireland, with its lack of connectivity to the Continent and dearth of mineral reserves, has simply made the most of what it has. In recent years it has conveniently skipped over the Industrial Revolution and headed straight for the intellectual, capital-intensive industries of the knowledge economy. A young, well-educated workforce (nearly half the Republic's population – 49 per cent – is under thirty-five, whereas the EU average is just 40 per cent), a competitive tax regime, membership of the single market and a huge hinterland in the United States has provided a potent mix (especially as US companies account for two-thirds of foreign direct investment into Ireland).

The Celtic Tiger years, from the mid-1990s until
the crash of 2008, saw the Irish economy soar, with
growth rates of 5–6 per cent a year. In 2005, The
Economist Intelligence Unit found the Republic had
the highest quality of life in the world, according
to the basket of criteria in its quality-of-life index,
beating Switzerland into second place (while Great
Britain only managed the twenty-ninth spot). The
boom – long, keenly felt and unprecedented in the
history of the Irish state – was, as all debt-fuelled
property booms are, built on quicksand. The fall,
when it came in 2008, was precipitous and painful.
As *The Economist* put it: 'Output from peak to trough
fell by 21% in nominal terms and unemployment
rose from 5% to 15%. As house prices plummeted
by 47%, the banks collapsed and had to be rescued,
which pushed the debt-to-GDP ratio to 123%.'[16]

In 2010, the Irish government accepted (under
duress) an €85 billion bailout programme from the
European Central Bank, the European Commission and International Monetary Fund. The Troika's

---

16   Quoted in *The Economist*, 22 February 2014.

'assistance for austerity' terms forced the Irish government into three years of painful retrenchment in order to recapitalise its banks and rebalance its public finances. In December 2013, Ireland exited the bailout programme, becoming the first of the financially distressed Eurozone members to do so (and in the process, a poster boy for euro-austerity).

Fine Gael Taoiseach Enda Kenny, who inherited the deal upon winning the 2011 general election and made many of the savage cuts required, actually made a televised address to the country to confirm Ireland was ending the programme early. He said that Ireland's 'good name' had been restored and that its future direction would be based on 'enterprise, not on greed', while the banking system would have to become a 'contributor rather than a huge drain [on the economy]'. Meanwhile, his Finance Minister, Michael Noonan, said that ordinary Irish citizens were the 'real heroes and heroines' of the story, describing the financial crisis as the worst Ireland had faced since the Famine. Indeed, they were. As the Irish economist Paul Sweeney put it, Ireland lost 'almost a decade of economic progress'.

So Ireland has been through the grinder in recent years. Yet, even amid the equivalent of extreme boot camp to deal with its debt and banking problems, some of its other economic and financial fundamentals remained in robust health. In May 2016, the IMD World Competitiveness Center (IMDWCC), a think tank measuring nations' relative economic competitiveness, reported Ireland moving from sixteenth position out of sixty-one advanced nations in 2015, to seventh position in 2016 (Britain was eighteenth). In its assessment of sub-categories, the IMDWCC found Ireland was actually first for 'Real GDP Growth', 'Flexibility and adaptability of people', 'Real GDP Growth per capita', 'Investment Incentives', 'National Culture' and 'Finance Skills'. As clean bills of health go, it was pretty emphatic and evidence that Ireland is keen to get back down to business. (Indeed, the World Bank calculates the Irish economy has been growing by around 2.5 per cent a year since 2012.)

A key ingredient in this success has been the Republic's record of wooing foreign direct investment. The approach became a cornerstone during the Celtic Tiger years, but the strategy stretches further back to the economic reforms of Seán Lemass in the 1960s. Indeed, it goes even further back than that, to Henry Ford, who was one of the first major foreign investors in the country back in 1917, opening a car plant in Cork, the birthplace of his father. (It is said that by 1930, 7,000 of the 80,000 inhabitants of the city worked for Ford Motors.)

IDA Ireland, the country's inward investment agency, continues this tradition. Its client companies have created 174,448 jobs directly, with an additional 122,000 created indirectly as a multiplier effect. The value of their exports is some €124.5 billion in goods and services and they pay €2.8 billion a year in corporation tax to the Irish state. After a brief hiatus in 2008–09, when foreign investment was hit, a familiar pattern has resumed. (Although foreign direct investment fell from 23.9 per cent of Irish GDP in 2009 to 10.5 per cent in 2011, it rebounded to 19.4 per cent in 2012, and during the period 2009–12, despite its problems, Ireland was still among the world's ten biggest recipients of foreign direct investment as a proportion of GDP.)

In fact, Ireland's record on foreign direct investment is so strong that IDA Ireland is planning to attract an additional 900 investments, generating 80,000 new jobs by 2019. In addition, it hopes to lever in €3 billion worth of Research and Development funding – double the current level – with the aim of spreading the proceeds of this bounty more widely around the country. Moreover, the top three export sectors for 2013 were pharmaceuticals and chemicals (28 per cent), computer services (22 per cent) and business services (12 per cent). This is not the agrarian idyll of John Ford's *The Quiet Man*. By 2019, IDA Ireland estimates that the numbers working directly for foreign companies that have been attracted to Ireland will be 209,000, up from 174,000 today.

It is this track record in attracting foreign direct investment that is driving demands from northern politicians for fiscal harmonisation with the south. They want a piece of the Republic's action. Northern Ireland's Department for Enterprise, Trade and Investment (DETI) calculates that adopting the same corporation tax level as the Irish Republic by 2018 will create 32,000 jobs by 2033. (However, having seen the cross-community Executive nearly collapse in 2015 over the issue of implementing welfare cuts, it seems implausible that things will pass off smoothly when it comes to plugging the gap in tax revenues left by a corporation tax cut from 20 per cent to 12.5 per cent.) Indeed, even when Northern Ireland lowers its corporation tax to meet the lower level found in the south, there is still a complication. As PwC found, in its 'Paying Taxes' report for 2016, the total effective tax rate in the Republic of Ireland, including profit taxes, labour taxes and other taxes, is 25.9 per cent. The figure for Britain is 32 per cent.[17]

And as the Hübner research argues, attracting foreign direct investment is not only about a competitive tax regime but also, 'and in many ways more importantly, about restructuring an entire policy framework to attract and feed high value-added enterprises'.[18] What is particularly noteworthy is

17 PwC, 'Paying Taxes 2016', 10th edition, p. 122.
18 Quoted in 'Modelling Irish Unification', KLC Consulting, August 2015.

that the keenest proponents of lowering Northern Ireland's corporation tax rate are Democratic Unionist ministers. They adopt this approach as the most business-friendly of Northern Ireland's parties, but the irony of seeking fiscal harmonisation with a neighbouring state they affect to have nothing to do with seems lost on them. This blind spot is, though, down to the entirely commendable urge to take greater control of Northern Ireland's destiny. In his 2012 conference speech to the Democratic Unionist Party, former First Minister Peter Robinson lamented that before the Troubles began, 'over 90 per cent of all expenditure by the Northern Ireland government was met by money raised here. And that should be our goal again.' Fiscal autonomy was his objective: 'Not reliant on the central Exchequer, but an engine of economic prosperity in our own right.' Robinson and his successors are surely right to argue for such sensible measures, but do they, as Unionists, realise the political ramifications of harmonising tax rates between two such small jurisdictions? Such integrative logic only ever travels in one direction.

Yet, it is perhaps further proof that economics will overtake Northern Ireland's stalled politics and deliver a form of economic unity before we see its political equivalent catch up. The original dichotomy between an industrialised, urban north, pitted against an agrarian, pre-industrial south has been spectacularly overtaken in recent decades. In one key respect, the cities of Belfast and Derry are akin to many northern English cities and towns in having undergone a structural economic decline, spurred on by the demise of traditional sectors and their replacement with lower-value, more insecure service industry work.

Meanwhile, the command and control economics of partition and the Troubles – all military spending and insurance underwriting of terrorist attacks – is now giving way to a more fluid arrangement, whereby the logic of a single, integrated offering in areas like tourism and attracting inward investment – as well as harmonising tax rates – are now mainstream positions to advocate. Capitalism is succeeding where politics has failed in modernising and redefining the relationship between the Irish and British states.

Dispassionate, hard-nosed commerce will gradually develop a single Irish economy, whether the politicians drive the agenda or not. This, in turn, renders the border meaningless. In certain respects, it already is. The various cross-border quangos established under the Good Friday Agreement to foster joint working are slowly seeing to that. Their very bureaucratic utility is a mark not of how peripheral unity is, but how banal. Again, it is small, incremental steps that will see Irish unity become a reality.

After all a state, like a human body, is held together by its constituent parts – bone, flesh and a central nervous system – each playing a role in the overall design. So it is with an economy, with trade routes, investment and shared infrastructure each contributing to a bigger whole. (Like the proposed 138km, £200 million north–south electricity grid interconnector project that stretches across the border, linking together power grids across the island of Ireland.) Formal cross-border cooperation is also happening under the aegis of the North–South Ministerial Council, one of the bodies established by the Good Friday Agreement. Already, there are a series of arm's-length bodies in agriculture, environment, education, tourism, strategic transport and health planning administering chunks of public administration on a whole-Ireland basis. Rather than have this happen in a piecemeal, uncoordinated manner, it is surely better to shape these emerging trends in order to maximise their impact. Indeed, it is irresponsible not to have the political and economic directions of these two small, interconnected jurisdictions properly aligned.

And given the integrative logic of the two parts of the island of Ireland cooperating and trading as never before, the process would seem inexorable. But why wait? Why not openly discuss where things will eventually lead? If we accept the logic that the Good Friday Agreement is not an end in itself, but, in all honesty, the prelude to fuller integration into the Irish state, then the responsible thing for the British political class to do is at least recognise this process is happening and manage its progression.

Something they failed to do with Scotland. Following the creation of the Parliament in 1998, Westminster took its eye off the ball (indeed, it was told

to the author by someone close enough to know
that Tony Blair regarded speaking to the First Minister as an annual chore). Scots came within five
percentage points of voting to leave the UK in 2014
and, given the state of the political landscape post-
Brexit, it remains entirely plausible that a second
referendum will be held at some stage in the next
decade. At the very least, there are complex economic issues relating to Scotland opting out of the
UK. Britain very much has a 'selfish, strategic and
economic interest' in its oil. Short of similar reserves
being discovered off the coast of Larne, Northern
Ireland is, in hard economic terms, eminently
dispensable.

After all, why should the hard-pressed British tax
payer continue to shell out £9 billion or so a year in
a direct transfer that sees Northern Ireland remain
one of the highest subsidised parts of the UK? For
every pound spent in the UK per head of population,
£1.24 is spent per person in Northern Ireland (it's
only 97p in England). Indeed, if devolving economic
levers and a bottom-up, what-matters-is-what-
works approach is the order of the day, there is only

one logical direction of travel for Northern Ireland: closer joint working with the south.

The business community is already leading the way, with Chambers Ireland and the Northern Ireland Chamber of Commerce establishing a 'formal affiliation' with each other. Welcoming the move, Ann McGregor, chief executive of the Northern Ireland Chamber of Commerce and Industry, said: 'By affiliating with each other our two organisations will provide a stronger platform and greater opportunities for interaction for all businesses on the island of Ireland.'[19] Again, commerce is leading where politics currently is not.

Yet, despite its many structural problems, Northern Ireland has, in estate-agent parlance, the potential to be 'an up-and-coming area'. In fact, the tourism pattern tells a more positive tale. The last available figures show a 12 per cent increase in visitors between 2013 and 2014 (possibly reflecting the international success of the HBO TV series

---

19   'Chambers of Commerce increase Co-operation to Support the All-Island Business Community', Northern Ireland Chamber of Commerce and Industry press release, 4 July 2016.

Game of Thrones, which is partially filmed there). Perhaps the most counter-intuitive finding is that Northern Ireland's tourism has, a few blips aside, been going up pretty much every year since 1985.

But Ireland wouldn't be Ireland without rain clouds looming. The potentially game-changing issue for Northern Ireland that will compel hard economics to prod the province's indolent politics is Britain's decision to leave the European Union. In March 2016, Northern Ireland's Department of Enterprise, Trade and Investment calculated the potential costs of Brexit, commissioning Oxford Economics to model a number of scenarios around the economic impacts of the UK leaving the EU. For the UK as a whole, it estimated a net economic loss in the range from 0.1 per cent to 4 per cent of GDP depending on the scenario. For Northern Ireland, the impact was more severe, with losses of up to 5.6 per cent of GDP.[20]

In short, if Britain catches a cold by leaving the EU, Northern Ireland will get flu. All the more galling

---

20 'The Economic Implications of a UK Exit from the EU for Northern Ireland', Oxford Economics, February 2016.

given there was a clear majority (55.8 per cent) of Northern Ireland voters in favour of remaining in the EU. Indeed, Northern Ireland was one of the only three regions/nations in the UK that did vote to remain (Scotland and London being the others). In fact, the Foyle constituency in Derry recorded the fourth strongest Remain vote across the UK, with 78.3 per cent support for staying in the EU.

In the aftermath of the Brexit vote in June 2016, the *Guardian* newspaper interviewed a series of business people in Newry, near the border with the Irish Republic. Declan McChesney is the third generation of his family to run Cahill Brothers women's shoe shop in Newry. 'Personally speaking, I am on the floor over this Brexit vote,' he said.

About 30 per cent of my business in this shop comes from the south and I am worried that if there is a crisis between the pound and the euro, will our products be too expensive for my southern customers? We have survived as a family business two world wars, the aftermath of the Easter Rising and the modern Troubles.

Now we have a new crisis that never needed to happen here after all that we survived. It is deeply depressing.'[21]

This vignette underscores the 'real world' problems that business in Northern Ireland will face as a result of Britain's self-ejection from the European Union. How will the resolve of the Unionist-led Executive fare when presented with a loss of EU funding, agricultural subsidies and regeneration cash, as well as the economic shock of leaving the EU and a flight of capital to the Irish Republic, where single market access is guaranteed? The obvious question is *cui bono*? It's fairly clear that England's difficulty is Ireland's advantage. IDA Ireland's homepage sums up the difference between pro-EU Ireland and Brexit Britain perfectly:

Ireland is a committed member of the European Union and provides companies with guaranteed access to the European market. Ireland is the only

---

21   Quoted in *The Guardian*, 24 June 2016.

English-speaking country in the Eurozone and provides an ideal hub for organisations seeking a European base. The brightest talent from across Europe is attracted here, mixing with our own to offer a multinational and multilingual melting pot of skills with a positive attitude to match.[22]

Subtle, it is not.

And all the more unnerving given Northern Ireland's record on securing foreign direct investment is much shakier than the Republic's. As the *Belfast Telegraph* reported recently: 'Northern Ireland had only 15 foreign direct investment (FDI) projects in 2015, fewer than half of the 39 it secured a year earlier, according to EY [Ernst and Young].'[23] Scotland had 119 foreign direct investment projects, while Wales had forty-one.

And this is before the effects of Brexit are factored in. It is, at the time of writing, entirely possible that a post-Brexit deal is agreed where Britain remains

---

22   Homepage at www.idaireland.com.
23   Quoted in the *Belfast Telegraph*, 25 May 2016.

inside the single market, with some sort of 'associate status'. However, it seems clear that would not entitle the UK to any of the other benefits of the EU, particularly the existing funding arrangements. These are significant and a report by the devolved assembly's enterprise committee in March 2015 found that quitting the EU would cost Northern Ireland £1 billion a year – equivalent to a 3 per cent fall in economic output.[24]

The report's author, Dr Leslie Budd from the Open University, argued that as well as damaging Northern Ireland's attractiveness as an entry route into the single market, transaction costs for trading into the EU would 'rise significantly' and inhibit economic cooperation with the neighbouring Irish Republic – a clearly not insignificant factor given the plans to harmonise its corporation tax rates with the south. Leaving the EU would also cut off vital funding that has done so much to copper-fasten peace in recent years. Between 2007 and 2013, Northern Ireland received £2.4 billion from the EU and continued

---

24   Quoted on BBC website, 24 March 2015

funding deals up to 2020 are 'central to Northern Ireland['s] economic and innovation strategies'.[25]

What are we to conclude from all this? Perhaps most obviously – that the economics of Irish unity stack up. There is now clear evidence that not only will both jurisdictions benefit from integrating Northern and southern Ireland, but it is an affordable and entirely positive move for both states. In pure public finance terms, Britain loses an unproductive long-term asset from its balance sheet, while the south gains in terms of scale and domestic market, buoyed by the effects of integration. Indeed, as the Hübner research shows, there is a 2:1 benefit for Northern Ireland joining with the south, putting wind into the sails of a newly integrated economy.

In this respect, the challenge is now laid down: why not realise the economic potential of a united Ireland? What is holding us back? It is time for politics to be as rational as economics. With Brexit posing very real risks to Northern Ireland's future prosperity, not least with the loss of EU funding and,

---

25   Ibid.

at this stage, uncertainty about single market access, there is no time to delay. Irish economic unity represents a pragmatic, evidence-based alternative model from the current, discredited, supplicant system where a manifestly unsustainable Northern Ireland economy swims against tides that will surely one day overwhelm it. Usefully, Hübner's research also concludes there is 'no established order' between economic and political unification taking place. He points out that in the example of German reunification, economic harmonisation came before political union. This means, logically, pressing ahead with fiscal convergence, something Unionists are strongly in favour of, but also developing stronger north–south ties around inward investment and infrastructure. It means accelerating cross-border cooperation ahead of Britain's departure from the European Union, which, whatever assurances emanate from Whitehall, will be a potentially cataclysmic event for Northern Ireland.

Indeed, as Britain heads into unknown political and economic waters, with the very real prospect, it seems, of a post-Brexit recession (certainly a period of disruption as our economy is reset), the economic deadweight cost of maintaining the status quo in Northern Ireland becomes less and less tenable. Indeed, if the economics of Irish unity stack up, the economics of Northern Ireland do not. A resentful English electorate, which increasingly eyes the public spending settlements in Northern Ireland and Scotland jealously, will simply not countenance the current arrangements indefinitely. Not when English devolution presents us with a cadre of powerful provincial metro mayors fighting for their share of the national economic cake. It would seem supremely unlikely they will allow the debate about the iniquities of the Barnett Formula to continue to be a closed discussion. British policy will increasingly find itself focused on levelling off some of the economic discrepancies created by Scottish devolution. Northern Ireland's bespoke problems will simply not command the same attention in the future as they have in the recent past. Ultimately, for British politicians, there are no votes in Northern Ireland.

So, what does a 'unity offer' or a 'unity dowry' look like? There are four key elements. The first is that the British contribution to the success of Irish unity should see sufficient funding put in place to secure the economic harmonisation that is necessary for the new Irish state to realise its potential. Realistically, Britain has a medium-term commitment of five to seven years before tapering off. This still represents fantastic value for the British taxpayer as a long-term commitment is taken off the books. As a key ally and export market it has an enduring stake in this transition working.

Second, this should be supplemented by the creation of an all-Ireland infrastructure fund. Public investment in Northern Ireland's infrastructure has long lagged that of the rest of the UK, so much so that Northern Ireland has among the highest smartphone usage in the UK because superfast broadband coverage is non-existent in whole parts of the province.[26] Annual capital investment in Northern Ireland runs at around £4 billion. Again, this is about half the figure for the UK per head of population (£2,173 for Northern Ireland, compared to

---

26 Federation of Small Businesses press release, 4 August 2016.

£4,292 for the UK as a whole). In contrast, the Irish Republic has invested heavily in its basic infrastructure over recent decades. (Last year it completed a ten-year €34 billion national transport investment programme.) It also has ambitious plans to develop a renewable energy portfolio and has one of the most advanced and competitive telecommunications infrastructures in Europe.

Third, the new Irish state should move quickly to realise savings from the de-duplication of public functions, freeing up money that can be immediately reinvested. The Hübner research puts this at 2 per cent of GDP in immediately achievable savings. Fourth, the integration of Northern Ireland and the Irish Republic secures ongoing membership of the European Union and the retention of access to the single market as well as current aid and grant arrangements. This avoids the looming disruption generated by Brexit.

The economics of Irish reunification are compelling. A plan to bring it about is eminently achievable. The timing is apposite. The benefits would be felt widely across the island of Ireland. The question is not 'whether' the economics of Irish unity work; they do. The outstanding question is how can politics now catch up and be jolted to respond?

CHAPTER FOUR

BUYER COLLECTS: THE SOUTHERN APPETITE FOR UNITY

The implicit proposition of this book is that the Republic of Ireland has a desire to accept the six counties of Northern Ireland as part of its state. That there is, in the parlance of eBay, a willingness for the buyer to collect. It needs to be said at the outset that this is a major assumption and deserves careful interrogation.

When asked periodically in opinion polls how they view the prospect of reunification, the Irish seldom speak as one. There are voices strongly supportive, there are those who see it as too abstract a question to merit much critical thought and there are those who sense taking on the place is more trouble than it's worth. Some display an instinctive kinship with their northern brethren, while others see them as actually foreign.

There was a telling episode during the official Easter 1916 centenary commemorations when the great-granddaughter of the socialist revolutionary and signatory of the Declaration of Independence, James Connolly, was upbraided for not being Irish enough by an irate member of the invited audience: 'I was told I was being disrespectful towards 1916 for talking through a song, that the event wasn't about me, that I didn't belong there with an accent like mine and that I should go home,' 29-year-old Sarah Connolly complained. 'He repeated [that] I should go home multiple times.'

The irony, of course, is that Connolly himself was born in Edinburgh and served, as a young man, in the British Army. A similarly insular, 26-county parochialism was on display during the 2011 Irish presidential election campaign. During one television encounter,

Sinn Féin's Martin McGuinness, one of the candi-
dates running for president, was assailed by a young
woman in the audience thus:

> As a young Irish person, I am curious as to why
> you have come down here to this country, with
> all your baggage, your history, your controversy? And
> how do you feel you can represent me, as a young
> Irish person, who knows nothing of the Troubles and
> who doesn't want [to] know anything about it?

Through the lens of British politics, it is possible to misconstrue the mood of the Irish Republic
towards reunification of the island of Ireland and
assume there is alacrity among its political elites to
absorb the north. It's nowhere near as straightforward as that because the mood of the Irish people
is far from straightforward, nor, arguably, has it
ever been. Despite the extensive commemorations
for the Easter Rising, it is often overlooked that the
original events of that week 100 years ago were not
immediately greeted with a popular surge of public support. Tales abound of how apprehended

Volunteers were marched through the streets of Dublin to the jeers and scorn of passers-by.

Yet, in the general election of 1918, Sinn Féin won three-quarters of the parliamentary seats in Ireland. Evidence, perhaps, that the Irish suffer from cognitive dissonance – holding two, mutually exclusive, opinions – in relation to how their freedom from Britain came about. A case of public respectability and private radicalism? Many – indeed most – Irish people would like to see the country reunified, but blanch at the methods that have, hitherto, been employed to bring it about. On the one hand, the prim and law-abiding Irish disown violence and criminality, yet the gun, as they say, has never been far from the ballot box in Ireland. A cursory glance at the antecedents of its political class bears this out.

Fianna Fáil and Fine Gael – Ireland's two largest parties – are the Romulus and Remus of Irish politics. Although Sinn Féin is actually the oldest political party on the island of Ireland and the Irish Labour Party (formed by James Connolly) is very nearly as old, it is Fianna Fáil and Fine Gael that have proven the most electorally potent. Hard to categorise in purely left/right terms (and hard, even, for British audiences to pronounce), both are Nationalist and support free enterprise, but with a social conscience. Fianna Fáil is the more socially conservative of the two; Christian democratic in nature, with stronger roots in rural Ireland. As it has shown governing Ireland for the past few years, Fine Gael is less Nationalistic and more free market and, these days, seems closer in temperament to an Irish version of the modern British Conservative Party.

In terms of their position *vis-à-vis* the question of Irish unity, both have impeccable Republican roots, reflecting the split in Irish politics between pro- and anti-treaty factions in 1922. Michael Collins, mastermind of the IRA's guerrilla war against the British, led the 'pro' faction that went on to become Fine Gael, while Éamon de Valera, a veteran commander of the 1916 Easter Rising, led the 'antis' and went on to form Fianna Fáil. In terms of their impact on Irish politics, it is Fianna Fáil that has governed longest and left the biggest mark on Irish public life and society. Roughly translating from Gaelic as 'Soldiers of Destiny', Fianna Fáil remains an avowedly

Republican party. The first aim of its eight-point constitution makes this clear: 'To secure in peace and agreement the unity of Ireland and its people.' The party's website explains that 'Republican here stands both for the unity of the island and a commitment to the historic principles of European Republican philosophy, namely liberty, equality and fraternity'.

Founded in 1926 by de Valera during a schism in Sinn Féin about whether to officially recognise the new Irish Free State and stand for elections, the fledgling party had, by 1932, formed its first government, moving to scrap the oath of allegiance to the British monarch that had been a requirement of the 1922 treaty. In 1937, the Irish electorate supported de Valera's proposed constitution – Bunreacht na hÉireann – which, *inter alia*, included a territorial claim over the six counties of Northern Ireland.

Not averse to tweaking the nose of the British for popular effect, de Valera withheld land annuities, stoking a tit-for-tat trade dispute with Britain until it was resolved in 1938 in an agreement that gave Ireland jurisdiction over three 'Treaty ports'

that Britain had retained in southern Ireland since
the foundation of the Free State. Protectionism and
populism were hallmarks of de Valera's approach to
politics, but taking control of the ports from Britain
allowed Ireland to remain neutral during the Second
World War.

Fianna Fáil governed Ireland for most of the 1940s
and 1950s, introducing key elements of the Irish
welfare state, before de Valera bowed out as party
leader in 1959 to be replaced by his protégé Seán
Lemass, a founding member of the party and, like
de Valera, a veteran of 1916. The pragmatic Lemass
is credited with opening up Ireland's economy in the
1960s, offering grants and tax concessions to attract
inward investment, bolstering Irish industry and
setting the country on the road to joining the European Economic Community. It was a radical change
of direction from the protectionism of the early de
Valera era, with its narrow interpretation of national
sovereignty. Lemass also sought to normalise relations with Northern Ireland's new Prime Minister,
Terence O'Neill, an initiative that looked promis-
ing until the events of the late 1960s spiralled out

of control. By 1966, Lemass had passed the baton to Jack Lynch. His was a difficult inheritance. Initially reluctant to run for leader, Lynch nevertheless provided a steadying influence in subsequent years as the Troubles exploded, both metaphorically and literally. (As for de Valera, he was elevated to become President of Ireland, a role he held from 1959 to 1973, dying two years later, aged ninety-two.)

During the 'Battle of the Bogside' in August 1969, as rioting engulfed the besieged Catholics of Derry, Lynch went on state television and, in a remarkable address, called for the United Nations to get involved, put the Irish Army on standby along the border and urged the British government to begin serious talks about Irish unity:

> It is clear now that the present situation cannot be allowed to continue. It is evident also that the Stormont government is no longer in control of the situation. Indeed, the present situation is the inevitable outcome of the policies pursued for decades by successive Stormont governments. It is clear also that the Irish government

can no longer stand by and see innocent people injured and perhaps worse. It is obvious that the RUC is no longer accepted as an impartial police force. Neither would the employment of British troops be acceptable nor would they be likely to restore peaceful conditions, certainly not in the long term.[27]

In a brilliant piece of political *schadenfreude*, he urged British ministers to 'apply immediately to the United Nations for the urgent dispatch of a peace-keeping force to the Six Counties of Northern Ireland'. And demanded that they 'see to it that police attacks on the people of Derry should cease immediately'.

However, Lynch's *coup de grâce* was to come:

Very many people have been injured and some of them seriously. We know that many of these do not wish to be treated in Six County hospitals.

---

27 www.rte.ie/archives/exhibition/1042-northern-ireland-1969/
1048-august-1969/320416-broadcast-by-an-taoiseach/

We have, therefore, directed the Irish Army authorities to have field hospitals established in County Donegal adjacent to Derry and at other points along the border where they may be necessary.[28]

At once assertive and highly evocative, it was also deliberately aimed at embarrassing the Northern Irish and British authorities. Nearly fifty years later, the address is still startling and a mark of how poor Anglo-Irish relations were for so long. Indeed, as Lynch concluded, Irish unity represented 'the only permanent solution for the problem ... [It] is our intention to request the British government to enter into early negotiations with the Irish government to review the present constitutional position of the Six Counties of Northern Ireland.'[29]

In trying to understand Fianna Fáil's political centre of gravity, it's worth viewing it as more of a Peronist movement, rather than a left/right political party. A national rather than a conservative party.

---

28 Ibid.
29 Ibid.

Patrician, populist, pragmatic and used to governing. It professes to represent 'the mainstream of Irish life' and, in a jarring piece of management speak on its website, claims to have a 'can-do attitude' with the aim of 'unit[ing] all in a common identity of self-confident Irish men and women in a dynamic, vibrant, prosperous nation'.

The party boasts that its electoral success down the years makes it 'second only to the Social Democrats in Sweden in its length of tenure in office'. As 'the single most coherent force in Irish politics', other parties in Irish politics 'have been characterised by their opposition to Fianna Fáil as their only common bond'. Modesty, it is safe to say, is not a trait the Soldiers of Destiny appear to have heard of. Yet it is this brashness, this ability to engorge whole tracts of political space, that has seen them withstand any move to embed more familiar right/left politics in Ireland.

Indeed, Fianna Fáil's emblematic support for Irish unity has, hitherto, degraded Sinn Féin's appeal in the south, since the Shinners decided in 1986 that they in fact recognised the Irish state and starting standing for election. Its 2016 general election manifesto – 'An Ireland for All' – contains a generous section on its analysis of where the political process in Northern Ireland is failing and provides measures to foster cross-border cooperation:

> The past five years have been marked by paralysis in Stormont and neglect by the co-guarantors of the Good Friday Agreement, the Irish and British governments. The pervasive sense of malaise that has sapped the potential of Northern Ireland can be seen in the degradation of north–south institutions by this government. There is a pressing need to re-energise the institutions of the agreement and build a lasting peace in Northern Ireland. We must ensure that the peace process is about more than just the absence of violence.
>
> Fianna Fáil always has been and remains, fundamentally committed to achieving the historic unity of our island in a single state. Unlike the indifference of this government, the issue of Northern Ireland will never be downgraded by Fianna Fáil. 'An Ireland for all' means a lasting, deep co-operation between both sides of the

> border building towards a peaceful, consensual
> unification of our land.[30]

So what of the chief rivals? Fine Gael is, electorally, the 'yang' to Fianna Fáil's 'yin'. Less successful electorally, their periods in office have been few and far between. Although more pro-market, pro-European, economically conservative and generally more circumspect on the question of national unity than Fianna Fáil, even Fine Gael's 2016 manifesto committed the party to

> actively fulfil[ing] the Irish Government's mandate
> as a coguarantor of the Good Friday Agreement
> and, building on the substantial progress already
> made, will honour commitments under subsequent agreements including the 2014 Stormont
> House and the 2015 Fresh Start Agreement, which
> together provide a new political, social and economic framework for Northern Ireland.[31]

---

30 Fianna Fáil General Election Manifesto 2016.
31 Fine Gael General Election Manifesto 2016.

Similarly, the Irish Labour Party, formed by James Connolly in 1912, and frequently a junior coalition partner for either Fine Gael or Fianna Fáil, stood on a manifesto in 2016 of wanting to 'commence a national conversation about the future of our island and within it our many diverse communities'. It added:

> Labour is fully committed to supporting the institutions and spirit of the Good Friday Agreement to ensure stability and peace in Northern Ireland. We also believe in fostering a mature dialogue between every community, north and south, on how we can best secure the long-term prosperity of our shared island. We do not believe the barriers of the past should stand in the way of considering a better future.[32]

Viewed cynically, Fianna Fáil has traditionally fulfilled the desire for a 32-county Republic while doing little to actually bring it about. This has suited

---

32 Irish Labour Party General Election Manifesto 2016.

the Irish, who are free to maintain their emotional connection with the idea of national reunification without having to worry about the practicalities of it ever happening. Indeed, Fianna Fáil governments have often been eye-wateringly brutal in their treatment of Irish Republicans from the time of the Civil War right the way through the Troubles.

So, where is Irish politics today in relation to the question of Northern Ireland's sovereignty? The 2016 Irish general election saw 70 per cent of voters back one of the four main parties as their first preference: Fine Gael, Fianna Fáil, Labour or Sinn Féin. Scraped back to just those with an explicit support for Irish unity and Fianna Fáil and Sinn Féin drew in 38 per cent of the total vote. A further 32 per cent was divided between Fine Gael and Labour, parties committed to 'actively fulfil[ing] the Irish Government's mandate as a coguarantor of the Good Friday Agreement' (Fine Gael) while not believing 'the barriers of the past should stand in the way of considering a better future' (Labour).

It is surely significant that Irish political elites still feel the need to pay homage to the issue of national reunification, or, at the very least, commit to playing an active part in the affairs of Northern Ireland. And neither is it a fringe issue. Even newspapers actively hostile to notions of Irish unity, like the *Irish Independent*, cannot help but to drone on endlessly about the issue. The future of 'the north' maintains a spectral presence over Irish public life. Although perhaps the least 'green' of Ireland's main parties, Fine Gael felt the need to promise to hold the British government's feet to the fire in relation to Northern Ireland, by talking of 'actively fulfil[ing] the Irish government's mandate as coguarantor of the Good Friday Agreement'. As did Irish Labour, with its elliptical remark about overcoming the 'barriers of the past'. There is a palpable sense that 'the national question' remains unfinished business.

But where is the Irish public in all this? The first thing to note is that Irish politics (unlike Westminster) is not awash with polling data. Opinion polls are markedly less frequent, making the development of the public mood harder to gauge. Nevertheless, the last few years has thrown up a few serious attempts to divine Irish national opinion in relation to reunification. In 2015, the BBC and RTE carried out a cross-border poll which found that just 13 per cent of people in Northern Ireland want to see a united Ireland in the short to medium term, although this rises to 30 per cent when the timeframe is extended to 'during their lifetime' (lower, then, than the 36 per cent who voted for Sinn Féin and the SDLP, both explicitly campaigning for a united Ireland, in the May 2016 assembly elections). Among southern voters, there's a much higher level of basic support for the idea, with 36 per cent of people saying they want a united Ireland in the short to medium term (mirroring the 38 per cent of the vote overtly Republican Fianna Fáil and Sinn Féin managed in the 2016 Irish general election). This increases to 66 per cent of people when Irish unity is again framed as a longer-term issue.

Tellingly, support for Irish unity ebbed and flowed depending on whether it was deemed to hit voters in the pocket. In the Republic, the 66 per cent backing a united Ireland in their lifetime increased to 73 per cent if it meant paying less tax, but more than halved to 31 per cent if it meant paying more tax. In Northern Ireland, the 30 per cent supporting a united Ireland in the long term increased marginally to 32 per cent if it meant less tax, but collapsed to just 11 per cent if it meant paying more. As we saw in the previous chapter, there are now solid grounds to assume Irish reunification is an economic 'win-win' for both parts of the island, with the north benefiting twice as much as the south.

On the face of it, then, the poll is a disaster for those seeking a united Ireland in the short term, although, of course, responses vary. Among Catholics in the north, support for a united Ireland is at 27 per cent, but among Protestants it lags at just 3 per cent. But the BBC/RTE poll is interesting because it also captured support for the other constitutional options. It found, for instance, that 49 per cent of Protestants and 38 per cent of Catholics supported the status quo option: the current devolved assembly and Executive. While support for a return to direct rule from Whitehall (what we can characterise as further integration into the British state) stood at 30 per cent for Protestants and just 14 per cent for Catholics. On the face of it, this is strange. Why would more than two-thirds of Northern Ireland's Protestants not opt for a closer relationship with the mother country? Moreover, 15 per cent of Protestants and 18 per cent of Catholics didn't know which of the three constitutional options they preferred.

So, what we are left with is a range of sometimes incoherent responses offering little more than an impulse reaction to an issue that has yet to properly crystallise in the public's mind. Like British attitudes towards our membership of the European Union, which were generally positive only a short time before Brexit, there is something unreal about the public's responses until the issue to be decided looms into view as a real and imminent choice to be made. When voters are presented with theoretical options they respond theoretically. Campaigns count for a lot and the views of political and business leaders help to shape opinion. As no one is engaged on a sustained basis with the question of whether there should be Irish unity, we should not blame the voters for their mixed responses.

Perhaps, then, other polls taken after Britain voted to leave the European Union in June 2016 are more pertinent. A Red C poll for Paddy Power taken in the aftermath of the Brexit decision showed that 65 per cent of southern Irish voters would immediately opt for a united Ireland – a far higher figure than the BBC/RTE poll recorded. Support was evident across most regions and age groups, especially those aged fifty-five to sixty-four, with 70 per cent favouring the idea. More than two-thirds of working-class voters (69 per cent) backed Irish unity, rising to 71 per cent of Fianna Fáil supporters and 79 per cent of Sinn Féin's. (Although clearly high, there is a lingering question as to why these figures are not even higher given both parties are unequivocally pro-Irish unity parties.)

What both the BBC/RTE and Red C polls agree on is the significant baseline support for Irish unity among southern Irish voters. However, levels in Northern Ireland are currently not high enough to guarantee the success of an immediate border poll. (Although an admittedly self-selecting poll of 50,000 respondents in the Unionist-leaning

Belfast Telegraph in July 2016 showed 70 per cent in favour of unity.) However, the uncertainty generated by Brexit (set to run and run as a farce in British politics) may shift public opinion still further. If Scotland is anything to go by, once a referendum was clearly in prospect and the issues were widely discussed, support for independence grew and grew and, while not winning, the result was much closer than anyone in Westminster anticipated. As Gerry Adams pointed out when making a post-Brexit comparison: 'It used to be in Scotland that it was men in kilts with big beards that wanted independence, and then it became a real life issue.'

Will the same now happen in relation to Irish unity? Certainly Sinn Féin could hardly believe its luck that 56 per cent of Northern Ireland's voters chose to remain in the EU, but are nevertheless being forced out by the weight of English votes for Brexit. Their immediate call for a border poll on Irish unity was an obvious reaction that will, for now, go unheeded by the British government. But there is surely a sense in both parts of Ireland that something fundamental has shifted in the post-Brexit landscape. The age-old bid for Irish reunification now comes wearing neutral, utilitarian colours, responding to a genuine, contemporary threat.

Moreover, it is a call that has been heeded by the usually reluctant Irish establishment. Speaking at Oxford University in September 2016, Taoiseach Enda Kenny said the 'possibility of unity by consent must be maintained as a valid democratic option into the future',[33] while his opposite number, the Fianna Fáil leader Micheál Martin, called Brexit a 'defining moment in Northern politics' and 'hope[d] it moves us towards majority support for unification'.[34] This is the closest thing to a consensus among the Irish political class on the issue of national unity for many years. Indeed, when you throw into the mix voices from the global Irish diaspora (not least from those in British politics), investors who will continue to default to the Irish Republic rather than invest in higher-cost Northern Ireland (with its potentially lost access to the single

---

33   Quoted in the *Irish Independent*, 9 September 2016.
34   Quoted in BBC website report, 17 July 2016.

market) and with a British government remaining, in all likelihood, reluctant to make the case for retaining Northern Ireland (especially if sensing a realistic chance of off-loading it), then it is easy to see how public opinion might be channelled into a majority for unity in coming years.

The hypocrisy of many southern voters is difficult to explain. They happily vote for parties nominally committed to Irish unity without ever bothering much why it doesn't come about. An age-old pathology is played out. To support the cause of Irish unity is to validate 'the men of violence', which prim southern voters have always been reluctant to do; yet the same cause remains unfinished business to the very same voters; hence they are content to vote Fianna Fáil or Labour, or, increasingly, Sinn Féin.

Therefore, interpreting Irish public opinion *vis-à-vis* the reunification of the country is an inexact science. But how much greater would support for unification be if it were a live issue, openly discussed on both parts of the island – and on both sides of the Irish Sea? What if the prospect of unification was wrested from Republicans and became a mainstream position, embraced by all quarters of the Irish political class? Where would we end up? Would we develop a discourse that provided the practical steps needed to deliver a single Irish state? Would we quickly arrive at the cold, hard, rational case for Irish unity? Would we be able to consign simplistic calls for unification to the past and fashion a model based on practical politics and inclusivity?

When this moment comes – as it surely will – the case for Irish unity will not be about an emotional attachment to an abstract concept, but about presenting it as an issue of empirical good sense. An evidence-based proposition anchored in reality, not mythology or appeals to rectifying historical grievances. It's about a rational choice – whether or not the maintenance of two states, on a land mass half the size of England's, with a population smaller than the county of Essex, is a realistic long-term option.

The Hübner study makes abundantly clear the potential economic gains that can be realised for all parts of the island of Ireland by becoming one state. All that is missing, then, is the sustained political will to make this case – by both Irish and British political elites – in order to move this agenda forward. There will, inevitably, be resistance from Unionist ultras who haven't been paying attention to the direction of travel for the past twenty years, but for those bothered about their future standard of living, it makes sense to engage in the discussion. Equally, those parochial Irish (like the young woman who upbraided McGuinness) who have been blissfully insulated from the Troubles may cock their noses at the prospect of sharing a state with the querulous northerners, but they are each caught not on the horns of history, *per se*, but of simple common sense and capitalism's dislike of artificial borders.

It is untenable that the issue can be ignored any longer. The threat posed by Brexit risks damaging Northern Ireland's economy and will invariably spill over and hurt the south too. While the availability of another option – Irish unity – makes it an act of recklessness not to at least discuss a single-state option. In terms of public support, it is the shock of the new that drives voters to opt for the devil they know. This will not happen if the question of Irish reunification is on the table and openly talked about in a way that will serve to familiarise the concepts involved. All the more so if there were a 'pan-rationalist movement' for Irish unity. If the political and business elite, trade unions, civic leaders and academics said 'this is the right way to go', it would have a massive effect in normalising the issue and informing public opinion.

All of which is to argue that Irish reunification, moored in historical legitimacy, inspired by timeless values but fuelled by compelling economic and demographic forces, is the modernising as well as timeless position to advocate. It is not an appeal to the past, to a romantic Ireland of yore; it is an idea fit for the twenty-first century; of an emerging Ireland confidently meeting the world on its own terms.

CHAPTER FIVE

PUTTING AWAY THE CULTURE CLUBS

While peace may have broken out on the streets of Northern Ireland over the past two decades, another war is still fiercely raging. As political leaders struggle to deal with the aftermath of past conflict, history and symbols are these days used as substitutes for bombs and bullets.

Flags, marches and even the naming of a children's park have been weaponised in a game of cultural one-upmanship that leaves any onlooker from outside Northern Ireland wondering if people there have taken leave of their senses. But this is the natural residue of the legacy of Northern Ireland's sectarian strife, where one community has enjoyed and misused a position of power for so long and where the British state has chosen to allow that to happen. As a result, the cultures of Irish Catholics and Unionist Protestants are often mutually exclusive, used as cudgels – culture clubs – to bash the other side. Where the Irish speak Gaelic as a means of connecting to their ancient history, Unionists have adopted the cause of Ulster-Scots dialect to show that they, too, have their own separate culture and traditions. Where Nationalists paint gable-end murals of their heroes and martyrs, Unionists paint the kerbstones red, white and blue.

But here's the thing. The differences between Northern Ireland's communities, significant and often rancorous though they are, are more surmountable than many of the cultural differences that now divide Unionists from the mother country. Social attitudes in Northern Ireland exist in a parallel universe to the rest of the UK. Indeed, Protestant Unionists arguably have more in common with conservative Catholics than they have with mainstream

British public opinion these days. (So much so, in fact, that there were anecdotal reports that some Catholics actually voted for the Democratic Unionists in the 2016 assembly elections because of their staunch opposition to same-sex marriage.)

'More British than the British' used to be the phrase that summed up the bowler-hatted Orangemen; and indeed they were. But that phrase relies on notions of Britishness being static. They are not, and if historical bonds of mutual affection and tradition are what have held Northern Ireland in place hitherto, then these ties are now gossamer thin. This point is brought home again and again. On most touchstone social issues Northern Ireland and mainland Britain exist in parallel worlds. Gay rights? Northern Ireland is the only part of the UK where same-sex marriages are not legal. Abortion? Again, Northern Ireland is the only part of the UK where the 1967 Abortion Act does not apply.

Unionists know this full well and are quite happy that British norms do not apply in Northern Ireland. Take the Ashers bakery case. The refusal of a Belfast bakery to make a so-called gay cake celebrating

Parliament's vote to allow same-sex marriage in 2014 has turned into a surreal – and faintly comical – human rights issue. At the nub of it is whether a bakery owned and managed by a family of Christian evangelicals should be compelled to decorate a cake with a gay rights message on it for a gay customer, even if it contravenes their strongly held religious convictions. As the *Belfast Telegraph* succinctly put it: 'He [the plaintiff, Mr Gareth Lee] was seeking a cake depicting Sesame Street characters Bert and Ernie below the motto "Support Gay Marriage" for an event to mark International Day Against Homophobia.'

The refusal of the bakery to proceed with the order throws into sharp relief the issue that divisions in Northern Ireland are not neatly confined to whether you favour a united Ireland or not, or to which Christian denomination you belong, but between tradition and modernity in this deeply culturally conservative country. At the time of writing, the case trundles on, dependent, it seems, on the distinction between whether or not the bakery discriminated against Mr Lee deliberately because of his sexuality (they insist not and would happily sell him another cake) or whether they should have freedom of conscience to reject taking a job they found conflicted with their religious convictions. Guidance issued by Northern Ireland's Equality Commission skates delicately around the issue: 'If you are a service provider, it is unlawful for you to discriminate against your service-users on the grounds of disability, sex, gender reassignment, pregnancy and maternity, religious belief, political opinion, racial group and sexual orientation.'

So far so predictable, but it adds that organisations should not refuse 'to provide any of the goods or services which you *normally* [my italics] provide to the public'. Did Ashers normally decorate cakes with gay rights messages? It seems not.

However, in October 2016, the Court of Appeal found against Ashers's owners, the McArthur family, ruling that they had 'directly discriminated' against Mr Lee. Lord Chief Justice Sir Declan Morgan rejected the family's concerns about freedom of conscience, saying: 'The fact that a baker provides a cake for a particular team or portrays witches on a Halloween cake does not indicate any support for either.'

In any event, the case is slightly anomalous in terms

of Northern Ireland's culture wars. For starters, many conservative Catholics will be rooting for the family, conscious, perhaps, that their enemy's enemy is their friend on this occasion and any move in law to curtail freedom of conscience has deep implications for devout Catholics as well. The Ashers case is also about a contemporaneous issue – in this instance, the implications of the legalisation of same-sex marriages.

The more familiar cultural flashpoints concern the past, particularly what is remembered and celebrated. In such a historically aware and divided society, the sensitivities are everywhere. Indeed, 'one man's terrorist is another man's freedom fighter' is a concept that has never been more apposite.

Back in 2001, Newry and Mourne District Council named a small, nondescript children's play park in Newry after Raymond McCreesh, a 24-year-old native of nearby Camlough in County Armagh who died in 1981. He was also the third Republican to die after sixty-one days on hunger strike in the Maze prison in 1981. He had been jailed four years earlier for IRA membership, attempted murder and possession of a rifle used in the mass shooting of ten

Protestant workers in the notorious 'Kingsmill massacre', where ten Protestant workmen were pulled over in their van and shot dead by the IRA. Predictably, Unionist councillors and campaigners in the area have fought to have the name of the park changed. And, as ever with these issues, there is a seemingly endless process to facilitate complaints, appeals and counter-appeals. In 2008, Northern Ireland's Equality Commission called on the council to begin an equalities impact assessment into the naming of the park. Then, in 2012, Sinn Féin and SDLP councillors in the heavily Nationalist area decided to keep the park named after McCreesh. Two years later, the Equality Commission ruled that the naming was in breach of the council's own equality policy and recommended it review its decision. The council submitted a further report to the Equality Commission, voted to keep the name and the commission decided to take no further action. Then, in the face of legal action by the mother of one of the victims of the Kingsmill massacre, 88-year-old Bea Worton, the Equality Commission changed its mind and called for the council to discuss and vote upon the issue again. In June 2016, it advised the council that 'to ensure transparency, the Council debate and vote on this issue should be conducted in public and properly recorded and that Councillors should be provided with a qualitative analysis of the consultation responses prior to that debate and vote'.

Quite how many other parks across the United Kingdom are named after such forensic 'qualitative analysis' is moot; alas, it is an everyday case of Northern Ireland's circuitous decision-making. When all said and done, we are talking about a single children's playground. Yet the importance of culture and what the discordant communities of Northern Ireland choose to commemorate – or cultivate resentments about – takes precedence. The process becomes an immovable obstacle that retains the ability to undermine political progress. Doubtless it seems bewildering to British eyes. (Indeed, through those same British eyes, naming a children's play park after a dead IRA man is probably inexplicable to begin with and fodder for the confected outrage of the tabloid media.)

But think about it. There is hardly a town square

anywhere in England that isn't adorned with a statue to some austere-looking and obscure Victorian military figure. Come to that, how many Albert Halls, Waterloo Bridges and Nelson Squares – or permutations thereof – do we have dotted across Britain? Is it not equally likely that Irish Republican heartlands in South Armagh – the infamous 'bandit country', where the writ of the British state has long been tenuous – would choose to honour one of the ten hunger strikers? It plainly isn't to mainstream British tastes, but then Northern Ireland is hardly British, particularly this corner of it. For Republicans, it is Irish soil, which serves to make such symbolism highly potent, thus, commemorating Raymond McCreesh is entirely fitting. (Indeed, when it comes to the hunger strikers, it is not a trait confined to Irish Republican heartlands. Bobby Sands, the first hunger striker to die in 1981, is widely commemorated around the world, with streets in five French towns and cities named after him.)

But for Unionists, Northern Ireland is not really British either. In reality, theirs is more of an associate membership, benefiting from British taxpayers' largesse and attaching themselves to parts of British identity they like, while elevating their own identity and cultural associations to greater importance. This conditional attachment gives rise to the quip that they are not so much loyal to the Crown as the half-crown. To Unionists, Edward Carson remains the lion of Unionism, the implacable opponent of Home Rule and first signatory of the 1912 Ulster Covenant. However, to many Brits, he was the Marquis of Queensbury's merciless barrister pulverising poor Oscar Wilde in his infamous libel battle. Little of Unionism's very specific cultural identity is now shared with the British. Most obviously, the hyper-religiosity of many evangelical Protestants is seriously out of kilter with the post-religious British. Likewise, there was little of Unionism's skirt-hitching in British politics at the prospects of seeing Sinn Féin in government, or about paramilitary prisoner releases, following the signing of the Good Friday Agreement. Even on the sporting field we are separate tribes. Most Unionists are full-throated supporters of the all-Ireland rugby and cricket teams and Northern Ireland's football team, while the UK's Olympics team is referred to as 'Team GB' – omitting any reference to Northern Ireland at all.

So, when it comes to defending their cultural turf, Unionists have little trust in the mechanisms put in place for policing disputes about the rights of identity. However, particular ire is reserved for the Parades Commission – surely the strangest quango in the British state – which determines whether contentious public marches can go ahead. Invariably, these are Orange Order marches (and always marches, never 'parades'), earning Unionist scorn for curtailing their 'right' to traverse the Queen's Highway wherever and whenever they choose. Similarly, the Equality Commission is seen as another hostile redoubt of politically correct anti-Unionism, pursuing the Ashers bakery case and failing, as Unionists see it, to rule decisively against the Raymond McCreesh park. Indeed, the son of Bea Worton, who brought the successful complaint to the Equality Commission, accused the body of seeking to 'ride two horses'. He added: 'They have come down very hard on Ashers bakery in comparison to McCreesh Park, but I feel this case is much more important. They initially came out very strongly against the McCreesh name but later did somersaults to conclude that they had no power to overturn it.'

Chronicling Northern Ireland's brittle identity politics would merit its own book. There are some genuinely important issues about how a divided society learns to live together and forges a new shared politics amid the infernal tit-for-tattery. Again, however, British observers know and care little for these nuances and micro-grievances. But that's because ignoring history and hoping the past goes away is a particularly British trait. For the Irish – whether of the Green or Orange persuasion – history is essential. It links, in an instant, their contemporaneous identity with a specific time and place in the past. In all likelihood, a victory or grievance. Northern Ireland can no more forget its history – or 'move on' in the parlance of confessional daytime television – than it can forget about the weather. It's just there. Felt by all. Yet it's perceived differently.

So how, then, do you de-escalate a culture war? Can you? Is it possible to find common ground – a shared narrative – between binary identities that have spent so long as implacable enemies? Or do you accommodate both by trying to split the difference and create the largest area of cultural overlap? This is certainly the driver for integrated schooling. The theory goes that sectarianism in Northern Ireland can only be overcome by making 'the other' more normal and more recognisable. So if Catholic and Protestant children go to school together they will all grow up happily together, in a spirit of comradeship and amity. It's a cute idea, but hopelessly naive. Religion is a badge of association, not the root cause of Northern Ireland's conflict. Marxist IRA men were not noted for rounding up young Protestant boys in order to teach them the rosary, or UDA types for espousing the theory of justification by faith alone to a bus queue of Catholics.

For political scientists, the Northern Ireland Troubles were an ethno-national dispute. In plain English: my side want this bit of ground to be part of this state, while yours want it to be part of another. Religion and culture add colour to what is, at root, a question of hard politics. So if we are effectively going to close down denominational schooling in Northern Ireland (while allowing it in the rest of the UK?), in order, we believe, to stamp out sectarianism, then why stop at schools? Why not close down Celtic and Rangers football clubs too? And ban the Orange Order? And close down the GAA? And rip down that statue of Edward Carson at Stormont?

Where do you stop? You cannot stamp out different cultures, nor the complex and volatile history that gave rise to them. What you can do is try to build another culture, working with the grain of what's already there and hope, in time, that the area of overlap becomes larger and deeper. This process starts with some mutual respect and perhaps toning down the moral outrage about slights, real or perceived, as well as the infernal 'whataboutery' that plagues Northern Irish politics. However, it also involves coming to a view about which aspects of Northern Ireland's cultural expression are valid and, much more controversially, which are not.

Take the most infamous example in recent times. The dispute over the flying of the Union Flag over Belfast City Hall in 2013 led to the attempted storming of the council chamber, rioting in the streets, a £20 million policing bill, threats to the lives of elected politicians and even an attack on Belfast's Lord Mayor. The issue began with a decision of the council to limit the flying of the Union Flag to designated days, rather than flying it every day of the year. And that was it. That's what the whole dispute was about. All that violence. All that animosity. All that public money simply because Belfast City Council took a legitimate, democratic decision to fall into line with every other council in the UK and only fly the Union Flag on designated days.

Of course, it didn't seem like a trivial issue to Unionists and their more militant loyalist brethren. Indeed, within a year of the protest starting, 560 people had been arrested and charged in connection with the dispute. Yet, away from all the fireworks, fury and gnashing of teeth, the Department of Culture, Media and Sport has clear guidelines about when the Union Flag should be flown. For 2016, there are twenty-one occasions when it is deemed befitting to fly it from public buildings. To be clear, these are not suggestions. They are not meant to be added to as local councils see fit. They are explicit.

Actually, it's even fewer than twenty-one. For

national patron saints' days, the flag is flown solely in the host nation. On St George's Day, the flag is flown in England, but not in Scotland, Wales or Northern Ireland. And in case Unionists think politically correct commissars at the DCMS have it in for them, the guidance for St Patrick's Day states: 'The Union Flag only should be flown.' Not the Irish Tricolour. As well as the Feast Days, the bulk of the remainder are royal holidays and special occasions like Remembrance Sunday.

In addition, the list also comes with highly prescriptive guidance about the positioning of the flag. For instance, the Union Flag should be flown on 9 May for Europe Day, but the guidance note states: 'Where the European flag is flown on this day, the Union Flag should fly alongside the European flag and, on UK government buildings that only have one flagpole, the Union Flag should take precedence.'

The very prescriptiveness of the list appears to have caught Belfast's Unionists unawares. Since 1906, the Union Flag was flown from Belfast City Hall each day – seemingly the only place in the UK where it was. This was clearly a mistake and it was entirely appropriate to bring Belfast into line with everywhere else. It is entirely valid to fly the national flag over a local government building, but only in accordance with the guidelines that pertain to every other local council building in Britain. Belfast, in that respect, is no more British than Bolton, Birmingham or Basildon.

In previous times, the issue did not arise. Belfast City Hall was a Protestant, Unionist citadel and did as it pleased. Over the years, as the population of Northern Ireland has altered, the stranglehold of Protestant Unionist culture has eroded. The row over flying the Union Flag was inevitable as the demography of the city, and, in turn, the political composition of the council, changed, with Sinn Féin now the largest party. It is a familiar pattern as Unionist hegemony is giving way to Irish Nationalist culture. And, while the particular row at Belfast City Hall has largely abated (protests in Northern Ireland never seem to end conclusively), the skirmishes seem to have moved into the suburbs, with complaints that loyalists are harassing communities in South Belfast flashpoint areas to fly the Union flag.

But, as David Cameron once observed, 'coyness' and 'reserve' are an 'intrinsic part of being British' rather than overt proclamations and displays of national identity. 'We don't do flags on the front lawn,' he once remarked. He was right: flag-waving is looked upon as a bit vulgar and excessive by the English. Better to flutter on the top of civic buildings than in people's back yards.

But in Northern Ireland, flags matter. Unfortunately, different flags matter to different people and for different reasons. To Republicans, the Union Flag is the 'butcher's apron' – a symbol of oppression and imperial brutality. To Unionists, the Irish Tricolour is the flag of a foreign country, one to which they insist they have no affinity – which is perhaps surprising (and a cause for regret) given its origins. The flag was presented to leaders of the Young Ireland movement in 1848 on a visit to postrevolutionary France. The story goes it was presented to Thomas Francis Meagher, one of their leading lights, who brought it back to Ireland and flew it for the first time in Waterford. Meagher explained its significance thus: 'The white in the centre signifies a lasting truce between the 'orange' and the 'green' and I trust that beneath its folds, the hands of the Irish Protestant and the Irish Catholic may be clasped in generous and heroic brotherhood.'

Some hope. Although the Young Irelanders – like many Irish revolutionary movements down the years – were led by Protestants, this history is exorcised from Unionist historical narrative. Men like Theobald Wolfe Tone, Robert Emmett, William Smith O'Brien and Charles Stewart Parnell – Protestants all – play no part in Unionism's self-identity.

Nationalists are more comfortable in their identity than Unionists, whose suspicions about being sold out of their birthright, as they see it, have been well-founded as political leaders from the time of Gladstone onwards have looked for a suitable opportunity to give them up as part of a comprehensive deal on Ireland. In contrast, Irish cultural identity, in computing parlance, exists on the Cloud. It is downloadable anywhere in the world; a truly global phenomenon. When the BBC World Service ran an online poll in 2002 to determine the world's favourite song, the winner was 'A Nation

Once Again', the elegant Irish Republican ballad written in the 1840s by Thomas Davis, another leading member of the Young Ireland movement (and another Protestant Republican). The verse invited the Irish to draw inspiration from the Greeks at the Battle of Thermopylae in 480 BC, taking on the might of the Persian Army:

> When boyhood's fire was in my blood
> I read of ancient free men
> For Greece and Rome who bravely stood
> Three hundred men and three men
> And then I prayed I yet might see
> Our fetters rent in twain
> And Ireland, long a province, be.
> A Nation once again!

Where Irish Nationalist culture – a mixture of language, dance, music, song, literature, traditional sports and the veneration of hero-martyrs – endures; Unionist culture, in contrast, runs to catch up. That isn't to deny there is a specific culture to commemorate, just that, for the majority of the twentieth century, Unionist identity has been inseparable from wielding political power in Northern Ireland. The two have been symbiotic; the state and its loyal garrison people were one and the same – where communal domination and entitlement went hand in hand. The erosion of Unionist hegemony in recent decades – spurred on by the forced equality agenda stemming from the Good Friday Agreement – has meant a reappraisal was necessary. Belatedly, Unionists realised that while Republicans may have decommissioned their weapons, they are still outgunned by them when it comes to fighting a culture war.

This doesn't deter some. The DUP's Gregory Campbell is Unionism's most enthusiastic nose-tweaker of Nationalists. In a long career as a culture warrior, Campbell has criticised *The Simpsons* for an episode about St Patrick's Day, berated the singer Dido for sampling a lyric from an Irish protest song, tabled a parliamentary motion calling for the car manufacturer Kia to change the name of a car model (the bizarrely titled 'Provo'), attacked the BBC for playing 'Roll of Honour' (a rebel song which had been rereleased to draw attention to Scotland's draconian legislation about the singing of protest songs at football matches) and was himself temporarily banned from speaking in the Northern Ireland Assembly after mocking the Irish language.

Rent-a-quote reactionaries aside, there have been grown-up attempts to address cultural issues. As part of the Good Friday Agreement, a number of cross-border bodies have been created to address specific all-Ireland issues. One of these is *Tha Boord O Ulstèr-Scotch* – the Ulster-Scots Agency, which is charged with the 'promotion of greater awareness and use of Ullans [the language] and of Ulster-Scots cultural issues, both within Northern Ireland and throughout the island'.

Despite these earnest efforts at inculcating a cultural even-handedness in Northern Ireland, older enmities have a tendency to ignite. Literally and on an annual basis when it comes to the Protestant marching season, the single most disruptive and divisive cultural event, which has frequently plunged Northern Ireland into political crisis and always leads to animosity, tension and violence. The centrepiece comes on 12 July as Protestants glory in the anniversary of the Battle of the Boyne in 1690, when King William of Orange defeated Catholic King James II.

Again, Britons observing this annualised ritual, where several of the most contentious marches are refused permission to pass through National- ist communities, are utterly puzzled to see night after night of stone throwing and aggravation, with Northern Ireland's militarised police responding with water cannons and baton rounds. And, while much of the angst around the so-called march- ing season concerns a relatively small number of events, this is of scant regard given the dispropor- tionate impact they have.

As mentioned, contentious parades are regulated by the Parades Commission, fulfilling its responsi- bilities under the Public Processions (NI) Act 1998. Its duties and functions include promoting 'greater understanding by the general public of issues con- cerning public processions'. It seeks to 'promote and facilitate mediation as a means of resolving disputes concerning public processions' and to keep itself 'generally informed as to the conduct of public processions and protest meetings'. The six commissioners, drawn widely from across Northern Ireland, are appointed by and report to the Secretary of State. Unionists would dearly love to see the Parades Commission scrapped. They see it as infringing their historic right to march wherever they wish, usually along traditional routes that may take them past Nationalist communities who at one time knew to keep their heads down, but who, over the last couple of decades, simply refuse to turn the other cheek while marching bands play inflammatory songs outside their homes and churches.

The Orange Order came into existence as a bulwark against Catholicism. It's something of an understatement to point out that it predates notions of political correctness. It may have been national news when Royal Troon Golf Club refused to bow to pressure and admit women to full membership ahead of hosting the Open Championship in 2016, yet the Orange Order makes it look like a gay Mardi Gras in comparison. Catholics are not only prohibited from joining the Order (although it's doubtful they would get much out of it in any event), but any putative member who is married to a Catholic, or has Catholic relations, is also banned. As you would expect, the modern Order does its best to finesse this point these days, citing its purpose as the 'defence of Protestantism' rather than the baiting of Catholics.

That's absolutely fine. The post-Second Vatican Council Catholic Church would no doubt find areas of agreement with the Order. (Indeed, it was Pope Alexander VIII who urged William of Orange to invade Ireland in the first place in order to clip the wings of Louis XIV, who was backing James I.) Although its numbers are in steady decline, halving since the 1960s to around 34,000 today, it is, for Unionists, an important element of the fabric of their identity, and there's no problem with the Orange Order continuing to exist. In fact, the Order's work in helping to remember and commemorate the fallen of the First World War is important and entirely worthy. The sacrifices of the brave men of the 36th Ulster Division at the Somme transcends their Ulster patriotism. Certainly, all freedom-loving peoples should thank them and remember their enormous sacrifice.

Despite the Orange Order's often noxious politics, it is an important institution in both historical and contemporary Unionism. Neither should there be any problem with their traditional Orange marches. All that is required – all that has ever been required – is for tradition to meet modernity half way. Northern Ireland is a pretty big place with a pretty small population. There's no shortage of places to march that won't cause friction. There should be no question, however, of passing through areas where they are plainly unwelcome, or playing sectarian songs as marching bands pass by Catholic churches. Huffing and puffing about their 'historic right' to do so shouldn't come into it. It's a question of give and take. The *quid pro quo* is that the Orange Order maintains its idiosyncratic traditions, but stays out of communities where it's not wanted. This is exactly how any contentious parade would be approached anywhere else in the UK. Of course, in a united Ireland, the Order would continue to exist and, in all probability, thrive. Already there are parades in the Irish Republic without any problems, like the annual Orange march in Rossnowlagh, County Donegal – the highlight of the Order's 12 July commemorations in the Republic – which includes representatives from up to fifty lodges from across southern Ireland, Northern Ireland and parts of Britain. The march has been taking place since 1900, predating the very creation of Northern Ireland, and provides an example of how Protestant Unionist culture can be accommodated in a reunified Irish state.

But it's not just Unionists who need to bend their principles in the cause of building a shared future. Nationalism, too, must show willing. How about a united Ireland joining – or, technically, rejoining – the Commonwealth? Having initially been a member, Ireland left abruptly in 1949 in a de Valera-inspired fit of pique. Might Ireland make common cause with the dozens of other Republics that have successfully prised themselves away from Britain by rejoining what is now a post-imperial networking club? Is it a threat to Ireland's sense of itself to make common alliance with the auld enemy over diplomatic niceties? This is, of course, a rhetorical question: of course it isn't. Indeed, there is a steady trickle of voices in Irish politics making the case for Ireland rejoining the Commonwealth. Irish senator Frank Feighan recently pointed out that thirty-three members of the Commonwealth are Republics and many of those have a large Irish diaspora. After all, confidence-building must work both ways and if it served to aid Unionists in preserving aspects of their identity in a united Ireland, then it is a small price to pay.

Deputy First Minister Martin McGuinness has certainly 'walked the talk' in this regard. His hand-shake with the Queen in 2012 during her Diamond Jubilee visit to Northern Ireland was the type of small gesture of normality that reverberates widely. (Fittingly, Her Majesty wore green for the occasion.) Perhaps the high point of McGuinness's cultural diplomacy came when he attended a banquet in 2014, in honour of President Michael D. Higgins's state visit to Britain. McGuinness, attired in white tie, was content to toast the Queen and stand for the national anthem.

In June 2016, he paid an official visit to the Battle of the Somme commemorations in France, laying a wreath for the fallen of the 36th Ulster Division and 16th (Irish) divisions. He admitted that as a 'proud Irish Republican' he was out of his 'comfort zone' but thought it was right to pay his respects to the fallen, representing, as he does, all the people of Northern Ireland as Deputy First Minister. His strategy of making overt gestures of respect towards Unionist heritage wins him few plaudits among hardline Republicans, but building confidence among Unionists that their culture and traditions will have a place in any all-Ireland dispensation is an essential part of normalising relations.

Alas, there is much more to do from the other side of the political aisle. Ulster Unionists were hardly in evidence during any of the commemorations of Easter 1916 – either those organised by the Irish state or community events in Northern Ireland. This was a lost opportunity. The official events organised by the Irish government went out of their way to be inclusive, going as far as to remember the British forces killed during Easter week. And, while culture and identity are potent sticking points on the road to Irish reunification, it remains contingent on all those who would see it happen to find ways of accommodating the various, often mutually exclusive, identities. This could see further gestures to guarantee and protect minority Unionist heritage (although Article 44 of the Irish Constitution is already robust in defending the rights of religious minorities: 'Freedom of conscience and the free profession and practice of religion are, subject to public order and morality, guaranteed to every citizen.').

One thing is clear: although Northern Ireland's cultural politics remain noisy and divisive, they are not a deal-breaker and there is a way of working past them. Ten years of cross-community working in the Executive, imperfect though it remains, is testament to that. Creating space to recognise and respect different identities and agreeing to accommodate or work around them is possible, if the political will exists to do so.

CHAPTER SIX

GOOD BUDDIES? RESETTING THE RELATIONSHIP BETWEEN BRITAIN AND A UNITED IRELAND

The Easter Rising, the week-long insurrection by Irish Republicans in Dublin in April 1916, triggered a sequence of events that eventually led to the creation of the Irish Free State and the establishment of Northern Ireland. It is something of a secret history to most people on the other side of the Irish Sea. This is remiss, given it also effectively symbolised the beginning of the end of the British

Empire. The total loss of control in Dublin, even for just a week, was a wounding humiliation for Britain. If uppity Nationalists could bring the second city of the empire to its knees, nothing would ever be the same again.

And, indeed, it never was. The event inspired countless other national liberation movements throughout the twentieth century. Everyone from Lenin to Mandela took inspiration from the Rising. Events across Ireland commemorating the centenary have stirred long in the psyche of the Irish. They should be remembered here too, with a measure of shame and regret for our failure to do the decent thing back then. Irish revisionist history (a version sympathetic to Britain) has it that, by the standards of the time, and taking into account we were midway through the First World War, the harsh treatment meted out to the main protagonists was no worse than what should have been expected. But tying the badly wounded trade union leader James Connolly, one of the main rebel commanders, as well as one of the signatories of the Declaration of Independence, to a chair in the yard outside Dublin's

Kilmainham Jail, merely for the pleasure of killing him by firing squad, was as disastrous a piece of public relations then as it sounds now. The price Britain paid for its wanton overreaction was to allow relations with the nascent Irish Free State to fester for the remainder of the century.

A free, independent, 32-county Ireland could have been the UK's staunchest ally throughout the twentieth century. So much pain could have been avoided – and perhaps more radical demands headed off – had Britain kept its word and legislated for Home Rule during any of the various attempts at doing so in the late Victorian and Edwardian periods. Alas, a specially reserved contempt for the Irish meant their yearning for nationhood was unlikely to see a resentful British establishment volunteer to make an honourable peace. Instead, we saw partition in 1922 and the creation of a sectarian state in Northern Ireland. The rest of Ireland was allowed to slip into civil war over the terms of Britain's eventual, messy, part-withdrawal. British elites cared not a damn until events in the north spiralled out of control from the late 1960s onwards. The failure to heed calls for civil rights from the Catholic Nationalist minority gave us 'the Troubles': the ultimate political euphemism for what was in reality a secessionist insurgency within the British state, pitting Irish Republicans against the British government and its loyalist vassals. The deaths of 3,600 people and countless tens of billions pumped into maintaining Northern Ireland's wretched stalemate seemed to stretch out for ever, until the peace process was encouraged to bloom from the mid-1990s and political statecraft superseded knee-jerk militarism.

What a different history we could have had with our near neighbour. The Irish playwright Brendan Behan once remarked that if it was raining soup the Irish would run outside with forks. But it is the British who, in reality, exhibit a maddening penchant for contrariness. An independent Irish state, born not from the bloodshed of the War of Independence from Britain, but from enlightened British self-interest, would, in all probability, and if properly accorded the respect of a sovereign nation, have remained a cornerstone of the Commonwealth.

Instead of Irish neutrality during the Second World War, Irish regiments might again have taken up arms for Britain, as they had done so successfully while part of the British Army for centuries before.

It took the state visit of Her Majesty the Queen in 2011 – the first to Ireland in ninety years – for these self-inflicted wounds to begin to heal. And heal they will. (After all, the Irish, as it is said of the French, are really monarchists pretending to be Republicans.) Meanwhile, our intertwined history, common language and large cultural overlap (*Mrs Brown's Boys* was, after all, voted the best sitcom of the twenty-first century by readers of the *Radio Times*) provide an ideal backdrop for raising the question of Northern Ireland's sovereignty. In large part, it is this renewed amity between these islands that makes Irish unity so inevitable, creating, as it does, a new political space free of the rancour of the past. So it is possible to believe Irish reunification is inevitable not in the way that, say, a Chesterfield United fan might hope their team will win the Premier League, but in the way a Liverpool supporter could envisage their side doing so. It might not happen this season, or next, but the day comes closer. It is, in short, an entirely realistic expectation. Previous form makes it so. As does the determination of those who continue to wish to see it brought about.

This is because the oldest political ideas turn out to be the most enduring, with Nationalism usually proving the most resilient of all. After all, until the last decade or so, it was fashionable in British politics to regard Scottish Nationalism as a busted flush, a fringe obsession. Globalisation and consumerism in our post-religious, post-ideological country consigned notions of popular patriotism to the history books. Indeed, the best place for such fantasies was the silver screen. Mel Gibson's Oscar-garlanded biopic of William Wallace, *Braveheart*, may have generated an outpouring of Nationalist sentiment among Scots when it was released in 1995, but this firmly belonged on the terraces of Hamden Park, not in the debate about a new devolved Parliament, operating within the British state, which was created in 1998.

Indeed, for the first decade or so following Scottish devolution, one might have thought Scottish Nationalism had indeed been caged. The novelty of having the Parliament seemed to sate all but the *Braveheart* tendency. Yet political ideas have a habit of emerging from between the bars. And, so, here we are in 2016, still trying to digest how Nationalists came so close to winning the referendum on Scottish independence in September 2014, before then flocking to the Scottish National Party's standard in unprecedented numbers at the general election of May 2015. In the process, the Scottish Labour Party, hitherto the staunchest defender of the link with the UK, was political obliterated, losing forty of its forty-one parliamentary seats to the SNP. The current assumption is that it's now a question of when, not if, there's a second referendum on Scottish independence. And a matter of when, not if, Scotland then goes its own way.

But will the Irish, faced with all the same siren distractions of modernity, reject ancient notions of nationhood in favour of easy living and the comforts of the status quo? The Irish writer Ruth Dudley Edwards hopes so. Writing in *Prospect* magazine recently, she argued that the Irish are 'too sophisticated these days to accept inherited myths uncritically'.[35] Revisionist commentators like her reject moves towards Irish unity with verve and use every opportunity to argue there is no demand or support for the idea. But the Irish are mercurial on the subject and there is a sense that polemicists like Dudley Edwards protest too much. She surely senses in the massive response to 1916 (nearly a quarter of the entire population of the Irish Republic attended a commemorative event over the Easter weekend period) that the question of Irish unity will never go away.

If we accept that Northern Ireland is in an antechamber; that Britain has no selfish, strategic or economic interest in remaining; that the economic logic of a single Irish state is compelling; that demographic changes are tilting the balance, making consent for unity more likely in the future; that southern Irish voters are less reluctant to take on their once-problematic northern siblings; then all it takes is for British and Irish political elites to accelerate these trends and begin to articulate that Irish unity

---

35 'The Fading Myths of Easter 1916', *Prospect*, 21 April 2016.

is the most probable and plausible long-term settlement. Indeed, the best outcome for the British people.

But then it always has been. Northern Ireland is an artificial construct. A territory founded as a political compromise, not for its inherent economic logic. And formed by the worst sort of compromise there is: the threat of violence. The Ulster Covenant, signed in blood, was a rather unsubtle prompt. Yet here we are, a century later, with two decades of steady political progress ensuring that Northern Ireland and its idiosyncratic issues and personalities will continue to drift from Britain's mind's eye.

The task, then – the responsible move – is to accept the overwhelming logic of the forces and trends marshalled against the current dispensation and to shape a new future by actively channelling them. Partly, this requires British and Irish political elites to 'deShinnerise' the concept of Irish unity and mainstream it as a sensible, workable and evidence-based position that wins support from across the political spectrum. The Republican model of Irish unity is but one variant. Other views should now come to the fore. One example is to adopt the model gaining traction in England with the current government's 'Northern Powerhouse' proposals. This might see Northern Ireland's principal cities – Belfast and Derry – given a large degree of control as powerful, semi-autonomous city-regions within the Irish state. Another model might be some form of joint sovereignty arrangement. (How this might work in the long term is moot, but as joint guarantors of the Good Friday Agreement, the British and Irish states effectively operate a form of shared authority already.)

This is because the Irish government has been afforded a consultative role in the affairs of Northern Ireland since as long ago as 1986 and the Anglo-Irish Agreement, signed by staunch Unionist Margaret Thatcher. The driver for Thatcher's diplomatic concession was principally motivated by the need to improve joint security, but the excuse is secondary to the effect: Britain was not able to govern Northern Ireland on its own and needed the Republic's help. This has developed into a special relationship, with every step of the peace process taken in tandem with the Irish government.

What do Unionists make of the evolving

relationship between Britain and Ireland? Their default setting in response to questions about Northern Ireland's constitutional status can best be summed up as one of 'nervy denialism' – forever suspecting the British political class is on the cusp of selling them out, spliced with a complete inability to countenance any change to their political status. Yet ambiguity is built into the fabric of Northern Ireland. The partition settlement in 1922 came with the promise of a boundary commission that would keep the border a live issue. There was even a long-forgotten referendum on Northern Ireland's constitutional status in 1973 (which Nationalists boycotted). There is next to no affection and little or no kinship between Britain and the Northern Irish Unionists. Churchill could scarcely believe Northern Ireland still existed by the 1940s. Harold Wilson described the loyalists who brought down the Sunningdale Agreement (an attempt at devolved cross-community working) in 1974 as 'people who spend their lives sponging on Westminster and British democracy'. Thatcher signed the Anglo-Irish Agreement over the heads of Unionists, while Tony Blair brought in the Good Friday Agreement that set in place the architecture for eventually transferring Northern Ireland's constitutional status.

To be fair to Unionists, some do get what is happening. Former First Minister David Trimble conceded in 1998 that Northern Ireland had historically been 'a cold house' for Catholics, given the rampant discrimination that took place before direct rule in 1972. But this is as close as we've come to a Unionist act of contrition for a fifty-year abuse of power.

Britain, however, has a relationship with Ireland and the Irish outside the context of Northern Ireland. There is the relationship state to state, the issue of Northern Ireland, and then there's the Irish community in Britain. There are few large towns and cities throughout Britain that do not have visible signs of successive waves of Irish immigration over the last century and a half. From the time of the Irish Famine onwards, the Irish have arrived on these shores in large numbers. To Glasgow, Manchester, Liverpool, Birmingham, Leeds and London they came. Usually to carry out back-breaking work on the roads, in the coal mines, or on building sites. Their legacy is the physical infrastructure of industrial Britain. It remains in the patchwork of social clubs dotted around the country. And in the Catholic Church, where Irish immigrants made up the bulk of the congregation until recent times.

It's difficult to accurately assess the number of Irish in Britain, certainly when you include the children, grandchildren and great-grandchildren of immigrants. There are around a million Irish-born in Britain, a figure that stays fairly static, but the figure for those with clear Irish antecedents stretches into the many millions. The difficulty with the Census (which has only had a classification for 'Irish' since 2001) is that it asks respondents to self-identify. Given the Irish are, in overwhelming numbers, Caucasian, it means that if you don't have an obviously Irish accent or surname, you can effectively disappear into the British population, hence, a systematic problem with under-reporting their true numbers.

And given the raw experiences many Irish faced with racism, especially during the Troubles, many parents were keen to impress upon their children that 'you're British now' as a means of shielding them from abuse. Of course, if you go back to partition and before, the Irish were not technically immigrants at all. With the whole island of Ireland under British jurisdiction, the Irish were merely British subjects. Therefore, to move from Cork to Birmingham was, theoretically, no more significant than moving from Leeds to Manchester. It was also the journey taken by a young Dubliner called Sean McLoughlin. A communist activist, he was a noted orator during the General Strike of 1926 before settling in Sheffield and working for the council until he died in 1960. His story is fairly unremarkable until you realise McLoughlin was the last rebel commander to surrender in Dublin during the 1916 Easter Rising, having been handed his position as Commandant-General of the Irish forces, aged just twenty-one, by the wounded James Connolly.

None of this is mentioned to imply the Irish in Britain is a reserve army ready to support Irish unity, but what it does highlight is that the reception in Britain towards Irish unity may be more benign that some politicians expect. That the sum of British–Irish relations is complex, three-dimensional and convivial and certainly amounts to more than the question of Northern Ireland's disputed status. Indeed, there could never be any settlement that did not recognise the close bonds of proximity, family lineage, mutual advantage and, yes, affection that exist between Britain and Ireland. It is a strong and enduring relationship exemplified by those who share their heritage between these isles. (Like the former Labour MP and navy minister Sir Patrick Duffy, a veteran of the Fleet Air Arm during the Second World War, who titled his memoirs *Growing Up Irish in Britain and British in Ireland*.)

So how does British politics approach Northern Ireland? As we have seen, generally, it tries not to. On the left of British politics, there has been an acceptance that the cause of Irish unity has a historical and moral legitimacy. On the right, a reflexive Unionism remains the default positon. But the urgency of addressing Irish issues has never held the attention of the centre of British politics. A political career in Westminster is not made by concerning yourself with Northern Ireland. Most MPs are happy to fall in behind the consent principle, that there will not be change unless a majority of people living there want it.

Clearly, the Conservatives remain staunch defenders of the Union and the constitutional status quo. But even their instinctive Unionism is perhaps not as rigid as it used to be. Back in May 2016, they were happy to back the Welsh Nationalists, Plaid Cymru, in a failed bid to oust Labour from control of the Welsh Assembly. And while the Tories are understandably pleased to have come second (a very distant second, to be sure) in elections to the Scottish Parliament (bloodying Labour's nose as they pushed them into third place), they know full well that there is only the remotest possibility of ever going one better. As a mainly English party these days, their Unionism is theoretical and aspirational and while they maintain a basic party infrastructure in Northern Ireland, they have no representatives in the assembly.

Back in 2010, however, there was an attempt to make a step-change. The Conservatives teamed up with their erstwhile allies the Ulster Unionists under the guise of Ulster Conservatives and Unionists – New Force (UCUNF). After the UUP's precipitous decline over the past fifteen years, from undisputed titans of Northern Ireland's politics (governing uninterrupted from the time of partition in 1922 to the imposition of direct rule in 1972), to also-rans, looking on as the Democratic Unionists have muscled past them. The effort was futile, winning none of Northern Ireland's eighteen parliamentary seats. However, to make matters worse, they actually lost the only Member of Parliament they then had, Lady Sylvia Hermon, who quit the party to sit as an independent in protest at the tie-up with the Tories (she's effectively a social democrat and closer to Labour). For a party that has a long attachment to maintaining Northern Ireland in the Union and which actually won the 2010 election (well, they came first in a hung parliament) to 1) have little voter appeal in Northern Ireland, 2) not realise this beforehand and save themselves the embarrassment of standing and 3) not at least win some brownie points with Northern Ireland's Unionist voters for at least bothering to stand, is surely significant. At the very least, it shows the Tories have no real feel for Northern Ireland nowadays and that voters there don't in fact much like them. No similar pact with the Ulster Unionists was ever tried again.

It was all a long way from the mid-1990s, when the UUP propped up John Major's government after losing its small parliamentary majority in 1996. This came at a crucial stage of the peace and political process, allowing them to exert a blocking influence on the nascent peace process that saw the Provisional IRA rescind its ceasefire in frustration at the glacial pace of progress, while an uneasy stalemate descended in the run-up to the 1997 general election. Things got moving once Labour won the election with a landslide. Tony Blair took a personal interest in nudging along the peace process, culminating the following spring with the Good Friday Agreement and a comprehensive deal around devolved power and joint, cross-community working.

Labour's relationship with Unionism has been difficult over the years. For much of the 1980s, the party was committed to a policy of 'unity by consent', seeking to 'persuade' Unionists about the merits of a united Ireland, until the advent of the peace and political process in the early 1990s, which saw the party fall in behind the consent principle – that there can be no change in sovereignty unless there is majority consent for it. It did so as an enthusiastic supporter of the Good Friday Agreement, one of the abiding achievements of Tony Blair's premiership (regardless of what people think of him for other decisions).

As the party of government, Labour assumed the role of honest broker. Overt support for Irish Nationalism was put on the back burner as the party became an enthusiastic guarantor of the peace process. So much so, in fact, that Northern Ireland Secretary, Mo Mowlam, received a longer standing ovation than Tony Blair at the 1998 Labour Party conference. Indeed, the view in the Labour Party in 2010 was that the Democratic Unionists could be persuaded to break for Labour in the result of a hung parliament. During the tail-end of the campaign, feelers were put out to try to make common cause with the DUP around the issue of future public spending priorities. Gordon Brown, in his capacity as leader of the Labour Party, wrote to Peter Robinson (after the civil service vetoed it coming from him as PM), guaranteeing that Northern Ireland's bloc grant would be left intact. Robinson was keen to present himself as a leader who could wangle the best deal from Westminster and had requested written confirmation from Brown so he could use the letter as a prop for a televised leaders' debate.

In many respects, this encapsulates how Unionists see their relationship with British politics. They are there to be courted. They will work with either left or right for the best deal, displaying equal suspicion towards both. The DUP sees its role as forcing Westminster to keep the public cash rolling in. As long as it is seen to be delivering, there is no scope for the hated UUP to gain ground. It also serves to illustrate Labour's basic approach about Northern Ireland: support the main parties and dole out the cash to keep things stable. Labour instinctively understands the politics of the pork barrel better than the Tories. The DUP knows only too well it would have got a better financial deal from Labour than the one it subsequently received from the Conservative–Lib Dem coalition government. Indeed, James Callaghan's government was kept afloat in the late 1970s by bartering tactical deals with minority parties, including, back then, the Ulster Unionists.

What of the contemporary party? Under Jeremy Corbyn and his shadow Chancellor, John McDonnell, the party is now led by two of Parliament's few, undiluted long-time supporters of Irish Republicanism. This has not gone unremarked, with taunts of 'IRA sympathiser' emanating from the usual suspects in the right-wing British media, the Conservative benches, and a good few barbs from his own colleagues in the Labour Party. So, in his first few weeks as Labour leader, Corbyn found himself refusing to condemn the Provisional IRA in a BBC interview and was even criticised for the fairly unremarkable act of sharing a coffee with Deputy First Minister of Northern Ireland Martin McGuinness and Sinn Féin President Gerry Adams in a café in the Houses of Parliament.

As a classic 'campaigning backbencher', Jeremy Corbyn holds radical views on a range of issues that sit outside the comfort zone of mainstream politics, particularly about the Israel–Palestine conflict and the broader Middle East. These are seen by his critics as emblematic of his naiveté about paramilitary organisations, raising questions about his suitability for high office. While many of his positions may not be particularly expedient in British politics (such as his response that Osama bin Laden's death was 'a tragedy'), his position on Ireland should not be included on the charge sheet against him. Two factors are pertinent here. First, was Corbyn's support for Sinn Féin and engagement with Irish issues throughout his long career legitimate or not? And, secondly, did it serve any useful purpose? It was certainly the road less travelled during the 1980s, when the Provisional IRA's bombing campaign in Britain was at its height, but it was entirely legitimate for Corbyn and others to take an interest in the pressing affairs of Northern Ireland, especially as we now know that Margaret Thatcher's government was itself engaged in secret talks with the IRA from the time of the hunger strikes onwards.

The problem is that Westminster has traditionally paid scant regard to events in Northern Ireland. It was, for too long, the British state's dirty little secret. Indeed, until direct rule was imposed in 1972, as the place literally went up in smoke, Members of Parliament could not even table questions about goings on there. It was legitimate, too, for Corbyn and others to have a point of view about events there. Northern Ireland is a zero-sum issue. When it boils down to it, either you are in favour of the maintenance of the union with Northern Ireland, or you favour Irish unity. It really is as straightforward as that. Indeed, Corbyn's position was, and perhaps still is, common enough around the party and in line with Labour's official policy at the time of 'unity by consent'.

Turning to the second question: has Corbyn's interest in Northern Irish affairs done any good? With the benefit of historical perspective, the answer is, yes, it probably has. Back in 1981, following the hunger strikes in which ten Republican prisoners starved to death over their contention that they were political prisoners, not ordinary criminals, Sinn Féin tentatively embarked on a strategy which would eventually bloom into the peace process. Bobby Sands, the first hunger striker to die, famously became Member of Parliament for Fermanagh and South Tyrone in a by-election while still in jail. This showed to Republican modernisers like Gerry Adams that Sinn Féin could graduate from being the Provisional IRA's front office into a distinct political force, eschewing 'armed struggle'. At the party's 1981 conference, its director of publicity, Danny Morrison, summed up the new approach: 'Who here really believes that we can win the war through the ballot box? But will anyone here object if, with a ballot paper in one hand and the Armalite in the other, we take power in Ireland?'

This twin-track strategy eventually led to Gerry Adams engaging in secret dialogue with John Hume, leader of the moderate Nationalist SDLP, in the late 1980s and the gradual creation of a space where Republicans could leave the gun behind. But it took time and a great deal of effort to switch this twin-track approach on to a single, exclusively political line. Engagement and encouragement, and, indeed, validation, of the kind offered by Corbyn and many others on Labour's left during the 1980s spurred on those in Sinn Féin who wanted to go down the political route. Indeed, without such support, the balance may well have tipped towards the militarists who were content to make 'the long war' against the British state even longer.

Like many on the left, Corbyn saw Ireland as a classic struggle for national self-determination against colonial rule. But he was by no means alone. Nelson Mandela may be the safest of safe options for any politician responding to the question 'who do you most admire in politics?' but he was also a strong supporter of Irish Republicanism. It was an association that weathered his transformation into international statesman. Indeed, Gerry Adams was part of the honour guard for Mandela's funeral. No British politicians or anti-apartheid activists were granted similar status. So, for those who still regard him as a dupe in sympathising with Irish Republicanism, it is only fair to point out that at least Corbyn was in illustrious company.

What of the other main British parties? Given Home Rule nearly broke them a century ago and it was a Liberal government that partitioned Ireland, the Liberal Democrats have remarkably little to add to current debates (although they are nominally twinned with Northern Ireland's Alliance Party). Their political forebears in Victorian and Edwardian British politics were obsessed by the issue of Irish Home Rule, not least because of parliamentary arithmetic, with Irish Nationalists a powerful and influential bloc in the House of Commons. Interestingly, the surge in support for the SNP in recent years (with fifty-four seats, they are the third largest party in Parliament) owes something to Irish politics too. Research by the think tank Demos argued that Scots with Irish ethnicity who historically supported Labour 'more consistently than any other group in Scotland' defected to the 'Yes' campaign in 2014's referendum on independence in large numbers and appear to have now stayed with the Scottish Nationalists, helping explain Labour's Caledonian meltdown.

Since partition and especially since the Troubles, voices calling for Irish unity have been few and far between. It is a cause that has been reduced to Irish Republicans (whose policy of abstentionism sees them refuse to take their seats in the House of Commons), a handful of Northern Irish Nationalists of the constitutional persuasion and some on the British left. It is an issue that has been siloed, deemed too unrespectable to support. Through the dark decades of the Troubles, this was logical enough. Labour MPs of Irish heritage will attest to the political risks they felt they ran in speaking out about the iniquities of British rule, fearful that the death of a British squaddie from their patch would play out disastrously for them.

That was then. Now, the landscape is different. Persuading Unionists about the merits of unity with the Irish Republic should become a mainstream position in British politics. Why not? To express a preferred solution is entirely legitimate, especially if it is hard-headed and evidence-based. Indeed, moves towards Irish unity are happening in a hundred different ways quite organically. The end of the Troubles has energised a range of forces – political, economic and social – that have, as yet, indeterminable effects. The one safe bet, however, is that the border with the Irish Republic will not serve to hinder any of these advances.

Here's one small illustration. Back in 2012, Simon Coveney, the Irish government's Agriculture Minister, addressed a meeting at the Democratic Unionist Party's annual conference. It was a reciprocal gesture between the two largest governing parties on the island of Ireland after Jonathan Bell, a junior DUP minister in the Northern Executive, spoke at the annual conference of Fine Gael earlier the same year. To the uninitiated, these are unremarkable events. But in the context of relations between the political elites of Northern and southern Ireland, they are seismic. Just a handful of years' earlier, no one from the DUP would have dared engage with a southern political party like that. Ireland was a 'foreign' country with no locus into Northern Ireland's business. Similarly, for a Fine Gael politician to voluntarily embroil themselves in the north's affairs would have been unthinkable.

What changed? Merely that normal politics ('normal' for Northern Ireland) has won out. Power has the effect of forcing statesmanship on those who would otherwise fail to adhere to its niceties. It compels decision-makers to be constructive. *Realpolitik* supplants gesture politicking. The price of power is that grown-ups must wield it.

The elections to Northern Ireland's assembly in May 2016 reaffirm this point. The flat, listless campaign saw almost a carbon-copy result from the previous set of elections, which, in turn, mirrored those of the election that came before it. The Democratic Unionists, together with Sinn Féin, effectively rule the place, with a few lower-ranking portfolios in the Executive usually reserved for the smaller parties – the Ulster Unionists, SDLP and Alliance. The predictability of the result and, hitherto, the absence of a conventional Executive/opposition split is seen by critics as a symptom that the system is broken. Actually, it's an indication that things are working well (even if the Ulster Unionists, SDLP and

Alliance have now given up their Executive positions in protest). Northern Ireland isn't a country in any conventional sense. It's a province and small enough not to be of strategic or economic importance to the British state. Its elections should be workmanlike and uneventful. We don't pay much heed, as a general rule, to the goings on of Kent County Council, yet with a population of 1.5 million it is only a fraction smaller than Northern Ireland. In 'normal' times, Northern Ireland would hardly register. The fact that it doesn't, at the moment, is surely a sign of progress.

The replacement of Peter Robinson with Arlene Foster back in January 2016 has also seen a subtle change of emphasis. As First Minister, Robinson clearly enjoyed being in charge, a reward for his long years of political idleness as Paisley's deputy. Foster, in contrast, a UUP defector and arch-pragmatist, missed out on the posturing of the 1980s and 1990s. Affecting Angela Merkel's unflashy style, Foster wants to get on with the job. In her leadership acceptance speech she rooted her politics in the pragmatic, focusing on 'ideas and not ideologies'.

The people of Northern Ireland 'don't want to hear their politicians squabbling about issues that seem unconnected to their daily lives', she said. Her 'deputy', Martin McGuinness (in reality her co-First Minister, giving rise to a description of their joint rule as 'Marlene'), has already shown a genuine willingness to work with Unionists to build trust and rapport, not only with Foster but with her two predecessors as well. Indeed, his unlikely partnership with Ian Paisley saw them christened 'the Chuckle Brothers'. This space to govern calmly and competently, with minimal histrionics, will only widen, creating the impetus to approach issues rationally and for politics and economics to progress.

Similarly, British politicians should not be hidebound by their historic inaction on Northern Ireland. If they do not want it to become an integral part of the United Kingdom – and there is not one jot of proof that they do – then the only plausible position is to become persuaders for Irish unity. Supporting the principle of consent does not render Britain mute. We, the British public, are entitled to an opinion on Northern Ireland. It is not enough for a declining number of Unionists in the extremity of the British state to decide for us. Not when the territory they would have us maintain remains heavily disputed. And not while it costs us £9 billion a year. Asserting a view about what is best for the British taxpayer is entirely legitimate – and decades overdue. The radically improved relationship between Britain and Ireland, and within Northern Ireland, sets the backdrop that now allows that conversation to take place.

CHAPTER SEVEN

HOW NORTHERN IRELAND WILL LEAVE THE UK

According to the Office of National Statistics, there are around half a million people aged ninety and above living in the UK. Of that number, around 14,500 are centenarians (270 of whom live in Northern Ireland). During the span of their lives, they will have lived through tumultuous change. Two world wars. The first human being to walk on the moon. They will have seen empires come and go, entire states come into being, before morphing into something else. Fashions – in clothes (as well as ideas) – will have changed and come back around again. Along the rich tapestry of their lives, meriting much less attention than many of the key global events they will have witnessed, remains one simple fact. They will have been born before Northern Ireland even came into existence.

At the time of writing, we are just five years away from the province's centenary. How will the place look by then? Two things will probably be apparent. The first, indisputably, is that it will still be a part of the United Kingdom, albeit in a period of transition that will see it eventually leave to become part of a new, single Irish state. The second is that it will be a far cry from the 'Protestant state' that William Craig boasted about. Of course, for most of the last century, that's exactly what it was; a fiefdom built on communal inequality. Over the last two decades, however, there have seen massive structural changes that have served to level the playing field between Protestants and Catholics, not least the Good Friday Agreement process and the disbandment of the RUC, but also the massive changes to the economy, notably the deindustrialisation of the economy and, with it, increases in urban poverty and decay.

Northern Ireland will appear to be hanging on by its fingertips – still the least economically dynamic or socially liberal part of the United Kingdom. People in Britain, a few staunch Unionists aside, will feel little affinity with the place. The Irish will, broadly, like to see their country unified, with guarantees that the economic impacts won't be adverse. As will Northern Nationalists (to reconcile historical grievances as much as anything else). Meanwhile, Unionists, as the name suggests, will choose to stay where they are, thank you very much; but will at least show signs of accepting there is a sizable minority of Northern Ireland's population that does want reunification, so they need to actually persuade Catholics of the merits of the status quo. Opinion in southern Ireland will remain passively supportive of reunification, while British political elites will maintain the pretence of valuing Northern Ireland – if pushed to do so – while doing absolutely nothing to stop it drifting, inexorably, out of the Union.

Of course, getting the north and south, Nation-alists and Unionists, to sit down and work out a shared future is akin to getting porcupines to mate, but it seems clear, given porcupines are hardly an endangered species, that they find a way to congress when we're not looking. We must not overstate the difficulties in persuading Unionists that their long-term future rests in a new single-state Ireland. As memories of the troubled Irish twentieth century fade, so too should Unionism's siege mentality. It simply has no justification in the twenty-first century. The Ireland they feared being appended to (well, if not 'feared' then certainly 'despised') and the Ireland that northern Nationalists hope to see are illusory in both instances. Bluntly, unity won't be as great as Nationalists think or as bad as Unionists assume. Neither should this be seen as victory or defeat. The more rational this discussion becomes, the more a single Irish state becomes the only credible long-term solution. And ensuring this discussion is rational simply involves channel-ling all the energy of the trends that are in play and transforming the political calculation about the best long-term settlement. In terms of British–Irish relations, the economic wins of creating a single Irish state, combined with the loss of a considerable item from the British state's public finances, means our relationship with the Irish Republic will be closer, more cordial and more mutually beneficial than at any time over the last century. Peace, progress and prosperity. Friends with benefits, if you like.

Modern Ireland's outward-facing, pragmatic, business-like demeanour is in stark contrast to the inward-looking, isolationist state that Éamon de Valera ruled. Indeed, the 1.8 million inhabitants of Northern Ireland should look south at the 4.6 million that live in the Irish Republic and see a better opportunity to shape their national future than they see peering across the Irish Sea at a mother country that has also now changed utterly.

The first eighty years of Northern Ireland's existence were founded on the antagonisms between the nascent Irish state and Great Britain, then among the peoples themselves of Northern Ireland during the dark decades of the Troubles. But when the rough edges of the relationship between Britain and Ireland are smoothed down, and when a similar process happens in the north, then the dynamics change and all things become possible. Ideas have a habit of slipping the leash. Yes, Sinn Féin wants a united Ireland, the SDLP too, but which party has been pushing most for fiscal harmonisation with the Irish Republic? The DUP, seemingly the least likely to recognise the move is what it undoubtedly is: the building block of an integrated single-island economy.

The push for 'ever greater union' becomes magnetic. Just ask the average British Eurosceptic. They will drone on endlessly about how the unelected European Commission drives the agenda, forcing the pace with a range of projects and initiatives that build upon the last advance, with sovereign governments left running to catch up. The point about political integration is that it is infectious. Why have a common market when a single market works better? Then why not have a single currency for your single market? And on it goes.

The same sort of process is going on in relation

to Scotland. The establishment of the Scottish Parliament did not end the demand for full-blown independence. It is clear now they actually provided a bridgehead for it, in a similar way, perhaps, that the Good Friday Agreement will subsequently do in Northern Ireland. Both are small, sophisticated countries with a hinterland in the English-speaking world; however, both are content to take their place in the European Union, with few of the hang-ups of the English. Both are knowledge economies with young, well-educated populations. Scottish Nationalists are showing that the oldest idea: national sovereignty and a people's determination to secure it, endures as a rallying point. Like the Irish version, it challenges Unionists to come up with a better reason to cling to the status quo. The only response is to offer the Scots more local control, which, in turn, makes full independence more, not less, likely. Indeed, this asymmetric constitutional settlement has triggered demand for the devolution deals across England.

The city-region model emerging in Greater Manchester, Merseyside, South Yorkshire, Birmingham and Newcastle is igniting demands for similar deals with southern county councils. Devolution is a ratchet. It only winds one way. It is hard to see how English devolution doesn't lead to the main city-regions of England becoming semi-autonomous from Westminster and Whitehall. The process also creates a local political class with a tighter focus on delivering for local people.

Something similar has happened in Northern Ireland. It's unlikely that, Martin McGuinness apart, anyone in Britain could name another member of Northern Ireland's Executive. Actually, you could extend the point to Scotland and Wales as well. British devolution has created a class of local political elites who are happily getting on with the job of running their nations without the vast majority of us noticing. This is fine. After all, devolution is the process of allowing decisions to be taken closer to the people they affect. It's also a disintegrative process and the fact we can scarcely put a face to those driving this process locally, be they Scottish, Welsh or Northern Irish, is now a fact of life in British politics.

All of which is to make the point that Northern Ireland is slipping out of the Union with little drama. There is no Machiavellian figure pulling the strings and manipulating events. We are merely riding a political zeitgeist affecting the whole UK, which coincides with the lack of interest the rest of the UK shows towards Northern Ireland, plus the availability of another viable model in Irish unity. It isn't 'great men of history' that will cause the break-up of the UK; it is the modest and the relatively unknown. As if to illustrate the point, the average age of the new Northern Ireland Executive is just forty. By way of comparison, Northern Ireland's first First Minister, Ian Paisley, was eighty when he assumed office in 2007. Half the new Executive was born after many of the key, defining events of the Troubles, like Bloody Sunday, internment and the Kingsmill Massacre – events that still cast their shadow over contemporary events. Indeed, the 32-year-old leader of the SDLP, Colum Eastwood, was still in secondary school when the Good Friday Agreement was signed in 1998 and had only just graduated from university when Paisley took office.

The Britain of the twentieth century was as markedly different from the Britain of the nineteenth century. So the Britain of the twenty-first century will be as different again. After all, it's Britain, with ten times the population of the island of Ireland, that has the greater capacity to evolve and change. In that respect, Ireland, with its combined population – north and south – of 6.4 million, is relatively straightforward. Britain contains multitudes, encompassing a level of ethnic and cultural complexity that should make your typical Orangeman rush to make common cause with your average Gaelic athletics enthusiast. There is far more that unites northern and southern jurisdictions of Ireland than now divides them, socially as well as economically. Those divisions that remain feel very twentieth century and increasingly surmountable.

That said, it is clear the Good Friday Agreement settlement – devolved cross-community power-sharing, the consent principle and the two governments acting as guarantors – is fraying at the edges. The decision of the smaller parties to forego their place in the multi-party Executive following assembly elections in May 2016 and set themselves up as an opposition party is symptomatic of this. Complaints about the DUP–Sinn Féin duopoly, which has a stranglehold on running Northern Ireland, are, perversely, a sign of progress. The place has transitioned from, literally, a war zone, to somewhere that sees people express fairly routine frustrations with their elected political elite. However, the emerging issue is how the longer term is approached. Here there is a growing need for clarity. What settlement does Britain want to ultimately see now the space has been created to approach Northern Ireland afresh?

At the moment, Britain resembles a landlord that will only give their tenants a six-month lease. The suspicion remains that they would like to take offers on the property. In this respect, the Irish state also needs to arrive at a clearer, more consistent view as well. Since the Republic dropped Articles Two and Three of its constitution, laying territorial claim to the whole island of Ireland as part of the Good Friday Agreement, there has been little said about the practical steps needed to bring about reunification. Mostly this has been down to an unwillingness to disrupt the political process in the north, but now is the time to discuss the issue openly. This time, the case is not even principally about politics, less still a 'victory' over the 'auld enemy'. The case for Irish unity is made in flat tones. More PowerPoint presentation than stirring graveside oration. This time, the argument is about utility – the practicality of absorbing the affairs of a jurisdiction that is still only the size of a large English county.

So how hard is it, politically, to unify the island of Ireland? What are the necessary ingredients? Clearly, agreement between the British and Irish states is a basic requirement, as is the consent of the populations of both current jurisdictions. But more fundamental than this is the intellectual assumption that the move is necessary. The belief in the inevitability of eventual unification needs to frame the thinking of political elites and people alike. So what drives these assumptions? How is a big idea generated and spread? Usually, it is down to long-term historical trends being all too apparent.

Change demands our attention. Take a case in point. Britain's tortured relationship with the European Union owes much to the postwar political elite's shared assumptions about Britain's declining role as a world power and the need to forge new alliances. The point about political change is that it is just as likely to flow from pessimism as optimism. While the end of the Cold War was the obvious catalyst for the reunification of Germany, and the expiry of Britain's territorial claim to Hong Kong was contractual. Both examples are instructive here. The sheer scale of German reunification in 1990, with the sixty-three million West Germans joined in a new Federal Republic by sixteen million East Germans was clearly a massive undertaking, dwarfing anything that might face the British and Irish governments. Meanwhile, the transfer of sovereignty over Hong Kong back in 1997 saw six million people transferred to Communist China, despite a clear majority wishing to remain in a democratic state. There was no talk of 'the principle of consent' during that handover. Sovereignty was solely a matter for governments to decide.

The UK's vote to leave the European Union in June 2016 is similarly game-changing for every part of Britain, shaking loose all sorts of questions about the UK's future prosperity and place in the world. The outcome was a patchwork of results, underscoring just how divisive the referendum experience was. Scotland, London and Northern Ireland voted to remain, the English regions opted to quit. The reasons behind that are moot. Perhaps cosmopolitan London, with its purring economy and high levels of inward migration, saw only the benefits of membership, experiencing few of the downsides that concerned voters in other parts of England. Why did Scotland and Northern Ireland opt to stay? Perhaps their historical connections to Europe make them more comfortable asserting their place among the other small but proud Member States of the EU? Or is it that they could be immune from the English obsession with being a great power? As smaller constituent parts of the UK, it is plausible they are more comfortable ceding aspects of their sovereignty? Or perhaps their pro-European-ness was merely an assertion of anti-Britishness (certainly among Scottish and Northern Irish Nationalists).

Their reasoning is a matter for the political scientists and cultural critics to mull over as the saga unfolds over the coming years. What matters here are the practical effects of Brexit on Northern Ireland. In a nutshell, they are profound and far-reaching. Let's start with the result. There was an all-too-telling split at the constituency level. Eleven of Northern Ireland's constituencies voted to remain in the EU with seven voting to leave, all of them held by Unionists. Two results stand out. In West Belfast, for so long Gerry Adams's seat and a Sinn Féin stronghold, 74.1 per cent voted to remain, with 25.9 per cent opting to leave. At the other side of the same city, in the East Belfast seat that was once Peter Robinson's political hinterland, the opposite result was returned: 51.4 per cent preferred to leave.

Usually peripheral to British politics, Northern Ireland played an unusually prominent role in the referendum campaign. Specifically, concern was repeatedly raised about the implications of a 'Leave' vote, given the north's land border with southern Ireland and, *ergo*, the European Union. The argument went that if Britain opted to leave, then the government would need to constitute a hard land border with the south – the new frontier with the EU – to avoid cross-border smuggling, illegal migration and people trafficking. A dystopian vision of watchtowers being erected at border checkpoints and razor wire unfurled across the green fields of Counties Fermanagh, Tyrone and Armagh was meant to ward off the Brexiteers. Alas, given Nationalists were already enthusiastic 'Remainers', the message was a classic case of preaching to the converted. It is also doubtful whether this idiosyncratic concern made much appeal to your average English voter. While Unionists – who voted in large numbers to leave the EU – were perhaps even enticed by the prospect of a hard border.

If so, they were deluding themselves. Rather than stymieing cross-border cooperation, Brexit will boost it. The vote to leave the European Union will provide the spur to accelerate the economic case for Irish unity. Why? Northern Ireland's heavy reliance on the EU for starters. When Britain leaves, who is going to pick up the bill? Who will meet the costs of all that EU farming support? Where will all that regeneration funding come from in future? The hard-pressed British taxpayer? What do Unionists imagine the British public will make of the province forfeiting the opportunity to 'wash its own face' financially by joining with the south, which remains a member of the EU and is eligible for all those benefits?

The decisions facing British ministers over the next decade: how to exit the EU on the most favourable terms, how to plug the UK's outstanding budget deficit, how to avert a second referendum on Scottish independence, and how to make sense of the creeping realignment of British politics, with the rise of the populist right and the travails of the Labour Party, constitute a toxic in-tray of difficult issues. There's little incentive to start adding to that pile by wilfully retarding economic progress in Northern Ireland. Unionists who voted enthusiastically for Brexit, imagining it would stop creeping moves towards Irish unity, have actually done the opposite. They have made the decisions of British ministers all the more straightforward. Further, deeper cooperation with the Irish Republic is now inevitable. All the more so because it represents the rational option. The sensible thing to do.

Brexit will change a whole range of assumptions and priorities in British politics. Investment bank JP Morgan has already advised its clients that it expects Scotland to vote for independence by 2019. Given 62 per cent of Scots voted to remain in the EU, and despite Westminster's dearest wish not to revisit the whole question of Scottish independence, Brexit makes it nigh-on impossible to avoid. Yet British politics is still reeling from the first referendum in 2014 and has yet to fully internalise the fallout from that near miss. That the issue now comes around again so soon – perhaps even forcing a fresh plebiscite in this parliament – is massively destabilising. Relieved 'Yes' campaigners hoped they had put the issue to bed for a generation. No such luck.

Again, a clear majority of Northern Ireland's population opted to remain in the EU – 55.8 per cent to

44.2 per cent. This tees up exactly the same issue as it does with Scotland: why should Northern Ireland be forced against its clear will to quit the EU and lose all the advantages of membership simply because the more populous English provinces choose to leave? It has its own impeccable logic, particularly as the referendum decision needs ratifying by the devolved authorities, making them complicit to a decision they passionately disagree with and, left to their own devices, would never have made.

So the UK's vote to leave the European Union in June 2016 is, plausibly, endgame stuff for Northern Ireland. All the hypocrisies and political indolence that serve to keep its constitutional status off the table now come frothing to the surface. The British government can scarcely be expected to plug the funding gaps that will now emerge. Instead, expect the conversation to start drifting towards talk of greater joint sovereignty with the Irish Republic. Unity will come wearing the clothes of 'partnership'. This course is easy to pursue on the basis that the two governments already act as co-guarantors of the Good Friday Agreement. As this book has argued throughout, the road to Irish unity is paved not with dramatic events, but with incremental moves. The shock of Britain leaving the European Union aside, what now follows are small, sensible measures that seek to make the best out of the difficult post-Brexit situation.

As mentioned, it is a classic case study in institutional integration, familiar to all students of the EU. 'Ever closer union' (to which the UK, ironically, has just chosen to extricate itself). Yet Northern Ireland is trapped betwixt and between the British and Irish states, fully belonging to neither, but with all political and economic reasoning now pointing towards closer cooperation with the south. What, then, might a unified Ireland mean in the context of Brexit? Most obviously it would see Northern Ireland remain a full part of the European Union. It would mean retaining all the existing benefits of being part of that union: most critically, agricultural support and regeneration funding and access to the single market. Little wonder, then, that there's been a deluge of applications for Irish passports – so much so there were reports that post offices in Belfast had run out of forms in the days following the referendum result.

Indeed, no less a figure than Ian Paisley Jr (son of *the* Ian Paisley), the Democratic Unionist MP for North Antrim, urged his constituents to avail themselves of the opportunity, telling his followers on Twitter: 'My advice is if you are entitled to a second passport then take one.' Casually remarking: 'I sign off lots of applications for constituents.' This may be a sensible, pragmatic response to Brexit, but it still represents a through-the-looking-glass moment to hear it from a Paisley.

But just follow the implications of people choosing to do this in numbers. We know from the 2011 Census that 25 per cent of Northern Ireland's population self-identifies as 'Irish'. You could conceivably see, then, a quarter of the entire population of Northern Ireland – some 450,000 people – not only choosing to assert a cultural affinity towards a neighbouring state, but actually choosing to become a citizen of it, enjoying, for instance, its diplomatic protection. This would see the Irish government hardwired into the affairs of Northern Ireland, if, for no other reason, protecting the interests of its citizens. Any spike in Irish passport applications would also compel the Irish political parties to take a closer interest in the reunification of the country.

But what if Britain does not, in fact, leave the European Union, courtesy, perhaps, of a second referendum? Or it manages to negotiate a deal which sees it remains in the single market? What then? All the same fundamental calculations remain. All Brexit represents is a shortening of the timescale in which Irish unity will be served up as the optimal long-term outcome for both British and Irish states. The direction of travel is still set. The economic benefits of Irish unity are still clear. Brexit, and the uncertainty it generates, merely accelerates these events.

Theresa May's elevation as Prime Minister may be another factor. In her introductory remarks from the steps of Downing Street after taking over from David Cameron in July 2016, she reminded the country that she leads the 'Conservative and

Unionist Party' valuing the 'precious, precious bond between England, Scotland, Wales and Northern Ireland' (as usual when such platitudes are uttered, Northern Ireland props up the rear, rhetorically speaking). Intriguingly, however, one of Theresa May's very first conversations as Prime Minister was with her Irish counterpart, Enda Kenny. He is pushing for the creation of an all-Ireland forum in order to make sense of the cross-border issues arising from Brexit. During the referendum campaign, May had intimated that it would be 'inconceivable' that Brexit would not entail the reimposition of tougher, physical border controls, but that was the campaign talking. Indeed, James Brokenshire, her new Northern Ireland Secretary, is a glass-half-full man, stating on his first day in the job: 'We don't want to see that hard border coming into place and I think there is a real sense of commitment between the UK government and also the Irish government to work together very closely so we don't see that returning.'

In terms of the broader issue of defending the Union, it is clear that Scotland will continue to do the heavy lifting when it comes to dissolving current constitutional arrangements. Nicola Sturgeon's administration utterly dominates Scottish politics through a unique combination of controlling the centre ground as well as appealing to the nation's radical soul. The SNP she leads has cornered the market in patriotism and radicalism and has adopted Labour's traditional position as the *de facto* social democrat vehicle of choice for the Scottish working class. A winning combination of mixed economy, social justice and pro-European internationalism. Fortuitously for her, Brexit provides Sturgeon with a convenient bogey to distract from any failings she or her ministers may accrue. It also provides an intellectually plausible reason for a second referendum much sooner than would have otherwise been justified. The effects on Northern Ireland of the ongoing Scottish push for independence are interesting. First, Scotland provides a useful comparator in order to amplify Nationalist demands for a border poll. It adds critical mass and normalises the demand for Northern Ireland leaving the Union (a much simpler and less costly exercise than Scotland going its own way, it has to be said). Usefully, the Scottish comparison also helps 'deShinnerise' demands for a border poll, allying it with a broader desire for independence fuelled by perfidious Albion's decision to strong-arm its smaller, more pro-European brethren out of the European Union. Moreover, it would seem to stretch credulity for Scotland to leave the Union and Northern Ireland to remain. There is a 'disintegrative logic' for Northern Ireland leaving if Scotland goes, given the historical and cultural associations between those countries are much closer than the connection to the English.

So what's the counter offer that Unionists – in Scotland, Northern Ireland and the UK – can now make to head off creeping demands for independence? More money and devolved power is already needed just to plug the Brexit-inspired shortfalls. Any game-changing offer to see off renewed demands for independence would need to top that. Do we know for certain that the English care enough about making it? If the next few years are set to be economically turbulent and with English animosity about the iniquities of the Barnett formula already evident, is ladling even more cash on the Celtic fringe something the English taxpayer will tolerate? After all, they have just opted to end an arrangement where they felt they endured taxation without adequate representation.

So far, no British political party has suggested it would acquiesce to Scottish or Northern Irish demands for a referendum to secede from the Union, but what if they did? Given their romantic attachment to the Union, it is hard to see the Conservatives (or the Conservative and Unionist Party, as the Prime Minister helpfully reminded us) changing the habits of a lifetime. Much the same is true of Labour. The party retains the hope of winning back lost territory in Scotland, vital if it is to ever mount a credible challenge again as a party of government. But what of UKIP – the third largest party in British politics, lest we forget, in terms of popular votes. They are already effectively an English phenomenon to begin with, so what if they decided to facilitate the national aspirations of Scotland and Northern Ireland – or at least did nothing to impede them – in order to spend more on England? We saw during the referendum campaign how potent an issue repatriating the £350 million a week (allegedly) offered up to the EU was to the campaign's success, particularly when earmarked for spending on the NHS. A similar pledge to perhaps spend more on the north of England, or in the south-west, recycling Barnett money that was previously spent on Scotland and Northern Ireland, would be powerfully resonant, tapping into English resentment at missing out. It doesn't even need to be a chauvinistic position, merely taking the Scots and a big chunk of the Northern Irish at their word. British politics is in denial about Scotland quitting the Union, while the prospect of Northern Ireland going barely registers. There is a massive void that a reenergised UKIP could usefully fill.

Such an approach is aided by the powerful moves towards devolving power in England (itself a response to the outcome of the 2014 Scottish referendum). Political power, as we have seen, is becoming more federal in a fast-changing British state. Enter UKIP making a pledge to spend more

on Merseyside, Greater Manchester, South Yorkshire, Tyneside and South Wales instead of the
secessionist Scots and Northern Irish. In any event,
attacking Labour in its backyard is the next logical
move for UKIP. Plus, the party needs a geographic
concentration for its vote, having learned the hard
way that wining four million popular votes does
not automatically translate into parliamentary representation in a first-past-the-post system. Perhaps
when British – English – politics fully internalises
the implications of Scottish and Northern Irish
desires for independence nothing will ever be the
same again.

In terms of Northern Ireland, consent should and
must be sought for any change of sovereignty. But
Britain need not simply wait for Catholic Nationalists to outnumber Protestant Unionists and hope
that the matter resolves itself. Seeking a consensus
over the reunification of the island of Ireland can
start as a minority position. (After all, the purpose

of this book is to try to explain not only the clear trends driving us towards Irish unity but the sparsity of debate in British politics about the entire issue.) It is up to the British and Irish states and their respective political classes to manufacture a consensus about change. To lead the debate. And to do that you first need to express an opinion. Indeed, the greater initial onus falls on the British political class to begin to discuss the issue at all. Rather than prodding a wasps' nest – the assumed reaction – they may find a British public that is amenable to the idea.

In terms of Northern Ireland's shifting demographics, we are five years away from the potentially irretrievable moment when Northern Ireland's Catholic population will outnumber Protestants for the first time ever. (The 2011 Census found 48 per cent of Northern Ireland's residents identified as Protestant, 45 per cent as Catholic.) The next Census in 2021 is potentially ground-breaking for Unionists' sense of self-identity. How will they react to their changed status? In 2011, then First Minister and DUP Leader Peter Robinson, in an all-too-rare moment of reflection, suggested that Unionism needed to reach out to Catholics and create a society where 'our place in the Kingdom is not reliant on demographics'. Indeed, Robinson asserted that there can be 'no greater guarantee of our long-term security in the Union than the support of a significant part of the Catholic community'. In post-conflict Northern Ireland there was, he said, 'a window of opportunity to reset the terms of political debate. We have the opportunity to secure our constitutional position beyond the visible horizon.' A nice sentiment, but there is precious-little evidence that Robinson did anything about it for the remainder of his time in office.

Unionists are terrible at initiating but adept at responding. Reform will not come from within. So this is the point when British politics should shake off the intellectual torpor that sees the issue of Northern Ireland's long-term future exist in a remote and long-forgotten silo. Actually, it's not even just the long term – there is no thought about the medium term either. How will things play out over the next five years? This will see the

British government trigger the Article 50 process that gives the UK two years to exit the EU. The exit itself is likely to be initiated early in 2019, meaning that, by 2021, we should begin to see the implications for Northern Ireland. No EU agriculture or regeneration money. An increased budget deficit (partly caused by cutting corporation tax to the level of the Irish Republic from 2018). Foreign direct investment continuing to head south given the Republic's continued EU membership and single market access. It is quite plausible that, by 2021, Northern Ireland will be in crisis, both politically and financially. Some centenary. What then? Will the British government simply step in and replace EU funding like for like? Will it plug the Executive's budget deficit? Will it continue to honour a funding deal that lavishes a fifth more on Northern Ireland, per head of population, than England?

Will the British public put up with that? Or will voters urge their political leaders to turn their attention to the choreography that resolves 'the Irish Question' and removes this painful thorn from the flesh of the British body politic once and for all? Unionists, plainly, will want no change. Some, perhaps many, will never reconcile themselves to it. Others might, especially if Irish unity continues to develop as a rational, evidence-based proposition that provides a compelling response to Brexit and the demographic paradigm shift in Northern Ireland and works with the grain of the massive improvement in Anglo-Irish relations in recent years.

For British ministers, Northern Ireland should be seen as an issue to manage out of British politics altogether. The next few years are shrouded in political and economic uncertainty and the concept of maintaining an expensive obligation to Northern Ireland, a place that we are not even willing to mount a 'first principles' defence of, seems perverse. Especially when there is a clear alternative model – Irish unity – that combines historical legitimacy with economic rationalism. All the more so if there are clear protections for Protestant–Unionist culture and identity.

In this context, 'persuasion' takes on a different character. Instead of trying to overcome the visceral animosity of Unionists towards a united Ireland, the issue is more about galvanising pragmatists – both Catholic and Protestant alike. Cleary, with such a bloated public sector, there are plenty of Catholic Unionists who currently put their self-interest in maintaining the status quo ahead of abstract notions of national self-determination. However, the post-Brexit economic landscape, the loss of EU funding and the reluctance of the British government to underwrite the costs of maintaining Northern Ireland mean that persuading them, on purely utilitarian grounds, that Irish unity makes sense has never been more realistic or achievable. Indeed, the next few years should see campaigners for Irish unity shaping an argument about 'proof of concept' – how Irish unity would work in practice – rather than making moral or historical arguments for it, or, indeed, waiting for the demographics to alter which might help facilitate it. Instead, they should point out that the economics already have changed everything.

Critics, however, point to the performance of Sinn Féin in the north and the lost seat and fall in the overall share of the vote the party received in last May's assembly elections. Unionists would love to think their support has now topped out, but they should be more worried about whether momentum towards Irish unity is not now a matter of big 'P' politics but a series of assumptions, among the business community and investors, for whom the border is an impediment to trade; among civil society, cultural institutions and a thousand other 'small platoons' that are getting on with their business, unencumbered by the artificial border across the island of Ireland.

So how do we get there? How do we arrive at the tipping point where Irish reunification moves from a dream to a real proposition? It needs to be talked about openly in British and Irish politics. To be sure, it's a long conversation about a short topic. There is no panoramic range of options. This is, ultimately, a zero-sum equation. Northern Ireland either becomes part of Ireland, or it remains part of the United Kingdom. It comes down to a question of whether we continue with Northern Ireland clinging to the coat-tails of a rapidly changing British state, ignoring the economic problems inherent in remaining (while disregarding all the benefits of leaving), or whether it takes up its historic place as an integral part of Ireland, transcending the pained history of the twentieth century to forge a new Ireland based on equal rights, mutual respect, tolerance of difference, freedom of expression and willing cooperation with Britain.

This 'unity offer' is set in an emerging context where relations between Britain and the Irish Republic are now better than ever and where the prospects of making a new constitutional settlement work for the benefit of all are real and genuine. It is now up to both governments – and the political classes of both countries – to begin articulating why Irish unity is the optimum outcome. The case for it will only become clearer and more urgent and there is surely a moral obligation to the Protestant Unionist community to stop 'stringing them along' when it is all too apparent that Britain has no long-term interest in remaining in Northern Ireland.

To be sure, there will be reluctance in Westminster. There is little willingness to be the first to point out the emperor has no clothes. But Northern

Ireland simply wasn't meant to last this long. It is right, politically and morally, to end the subterfuge that it can or that we should try to sustain it. Moreover, the Irish government should turn its attention to how the sinews of joint cooperation put in place from the Good Friday Agreement can now be strengthened to provide a basis for the administrative integration of Northern Ireland into a new, all-Ireland dispensation. This new polity will see the antagonisms of Northern Ireland's political class diluted in a 32-county Ireland, and with it a complete reboot of Irish politics; with new configurations emerging to replace the Nationalist/ Unionist cleavages in the north and the Civil War legacy politics of Fianna Fáil and Fine Gael. Irish unity is an invigorating, evidence-based proposition that is rooted in realism, not theoretics or emotion. It represents the best future for all the people of the island of Ireland and for the people of Britain too.

So what of those centenarians? By 2121, we may have lived through momentous events that aren't even apparent today. Britain's decision to leave the European Union in June 2016 was unexpected and dramatic and, as we have seen, has profound implications for Northern Ireland. By 2121, we should be gone. Likewise, anyone who thought the wave of Scottish Nationalism would recede once the charismatic Alex Salmond failed to secure a majority in the 2014 referendum on independence will have struggled to compute how his successor, Nicola Sturgeon, could actually improve the SNP's position at the 2015 general election and in elections to the Scottish Parliament in May 2016. The water level on Scottish Nationalism is not dropping back.

The larger point in all this is that the UK is disintegrating and no one seems equal to the task of stopping it. One thing is clear: the 'loss' of Northern Ireland will look like an after-thought once the UK exits the European Union and Scotland quits the UK. Both are far more significant. All the more reason, then, to begin the process of putting Britain's long-term, constitutional status in order. And part of that is discussing, planning, agreeing and implementing a proposal to do what countless British statesmen should have done in the decades since partition: reunify the island of Ireland.